Winning Divorce

Winning Divorce

Your Strategy for Protecting Your Children,
Your Money, and Your Property in Court

STEPHEN RUE, ESQ.

Award Winning, Best Selling Author

Winning Divorce: Your Strategy for Protecting Your Children, Your Money, and Your Property in Court

Stephen Rue, Esq.

FIRST EDITION

ISBN: 979-8-9951251-9-8 Hardback
ISBN: 979-8-9951251-8-1 Paperback
ISBN: 979-8-9951251-7-4 E-Book

Published by Must Book Press

DEDICATION

*To everyone holding this book with shaking
hands and a racing mind—*

the one blindsided by papers they never expected,

the one who stayed too long and finally found the courage to leave,

*the one fighting to protect children caught
in a storm they did not create,*

*and the one trying to hold it all together
when everything is falling apart.*

*You deserve guidance that comes from real
courtrooms, not guesswork.*

This book is for you.

GLOBAL DISCLAIMER

This book provides general educational information about divorce, custody, child support, spousal support, property division, domestic violence, substance abuse, and related family law issues. It is not legal advice. It does not and cannot guarantee accuracy or applicability in any particular state, county, or jurisdiction. Nothing in these pages creates an attorney–client relationship between you and the author.

You remain solely responsible for all decisions and actions in your case. You must consult a qualified attorney—and any other appropriate licensed professional—in your own jurisdiction before relying on or acting on any concept, example, script, template, or strategy described in these pages.

Family law varies dramatically by state and county. The procedures, standards, calculations, and remedies described in this book may not apply where you live. Before taking any legal action based on this book, consult with a licensed family law attorney in YOUR specific state.

Property division laws differ fundamentally between community property and equitable distribution states. The general principles discussed in this book may not reflect the framework that governs your jurisdiction. Consult a local attorney and, where appropriate, a certified public accountant or financial advisor before making decisions about marital assets, debts, or tax implications.

Spousal support and alimony laws—including eligibility, calculation methods, duration, and modification standards—vary widely across states. The educational overview in this book does not predict what any court will award or deny in your case.

Child support guidelines differ by state. Income definitions, calculation formulas, deviation factors, and enforcement mechanisms are jurisdiction-specific. Do not rely on general frameworks to estimate your obligation or entitlement. Work with your attorney to apply your state's guidelines to your specific facts.

Domestic violence laws, protective order procedures, and enforcement mechanisms vary by jurisdiction. If you are in immediate danger, contact local law enforcement or the National Domestic Violence Hotline at 1-800-799-7233. Do not rely solely on this book for safety planning.

Recording laws vary by state. Some states allow one-party consent; others require all parties to know they are being recorded. Violating your state's recording laws can result in criminal charges, civil liability, and exclusion of the evidence. Before recording any conversation, consult your attorney.

In many states, certain individuals are mandated reporters of suspected child abuse or neglect. If you have reasonable suspicion of abuse or neglect, you may be legally required to report it to child protective services or law enforcement. Consult your state's reporting laws and an attorney before deciding on documentation-only approaches.

Therapy is confidential, but it is not legally privileged in most family law proceedings. Therapists can be subpoenaed to testify about what you have shared. Be thoughtful about what you discuss with your therapist regarding your case, and consult your attorney about any concerns.

Financial information in this book is educational and general. It does not constitute tax advice, accounting guidance, or investment counsel. Tax implications of divorce—including alimony, property transfers, filing status, and retirement account division—are complex and jurisdiction-specific. Consult a qualified CPA or financial advisor.

This book does not diagnose anyone with any psychological, psychiatric, or medical condition. Descriptions of behavioral patterns are educational and intended to help you recognize dynamics and communicate more effectively with professionals.

Representing yourself in legal proceedings, even with limited-scope attorney assistance, carries real risk. Procedural errors, missed deadlines, and failure to preserve evidence properly can result in permanent loss of rights. If you are uncertain about any procedure, ask your attorney before acting.

If you have an attorney, that attorney's guidance takes absolute precedence over anything written in this book.

The purpose of this book is purely educational: to help you understand divorce dynamics, strengthen your preparation, and work more effectively with your legal and professional team—not to replace them.

CONTENTS

PART I: UNDERSTANDING DIVORCE: WHAT YOU ARE FACING

PART II: YOUR MINDSET, CREDIBILITY, AND EMOTIONAL STRATEGY

**PART XI: EVIDENCE, DOCUMENTATION,
AND BUILDING YOUR CASE**

**PART XII: SCRIPTS, TEMPLATES,
AND OPERATIONAL TOOLS**

INTRODUCTION

When Your Marriage Ends and the Fight for Everything Begins

The moment arrives differently for everyone.

For some, it is the day a process server knocks on the door and hands you a petition you never expected. For others, it is the morning you wake up and realize, with devastating clarity, that the marriage is over—that staying would cost you more than leaving ever could. For still others, it arrives gradually, a slow erosion of trust, safety, or hope, until the ground finally gives way.

However it happens, the effect is seismic. Your financial future, your relationship with your children, your home, your retirement, your daily life—all of it is suddenly in question. And the legal system that will sort through the wreckage operates on its own schedule, by its own rules, in a language most people have never been taught to speak.

For nearly four decades, I have stood beside people in exactly this moment.

STEPHEN RUE, ESQ.

Who I Am and Why This Book Exists

I am a trial lawyer. I have practiced family law for close to forty years. My firm has handled approximately five thousand family law cases—not five thousand consultations or five thousand phone calls, but five thousand real cases involving real families, real children, and real consequences.

Those cases have included everything imaginable. Simple, amicable divorces where both parties shook hands at the end. Complex financial dissolutions involving businesses, hidden accounts, retirement portfolios, and forensic accountants. And high-conflict wars—cases involving domestic violence, substance abuse, parental alienation, psychological manipulation, false allegations, and personalities so destructive that the litigation itself became a weapon.

I have watched a husband drain a joint account overnight and claim the money never existed. I have seen a wife forge her spouse's signature on a property transfer and deny it under oath. I have represented a father accused of abuse by a spouse who later admitted the allegations were fabricated to gain a tactical advantage in custody. I have stood beside a mother fleeing genuine violence who was told by her own family to "stay and work it out."

I have not heard secondhand accounts of these situations.

I have lived inside them. This is my daily work.

WHAT I'VE SEEN: The Husband Who Drained the Account at Midnight

---

Robert and Angela had been married for nineteen years when Angela filed. On the night she was served, Robert logged into their joint brokerage account and transferred $340,000 into a new account he had opened that afternoon in his name alone. He moved $80,000 more from their joint checking into his sister's savings account. By *morning, Angela's access to the family's liquid assets had been re-duced to $1,200 in her personal checking. Robert assumed the trans-fers would be difficult to trace. They were not. A forensic accountant reconstructed every movement within seventy-two hours. The judge imposed sanctions, ordered the full amount restored with inter-est, and noted Robert's conduct in the record—a credibility wound that bled into every subsequent hearing for the next two years. The money was always recoverable. The trust Robert destroyed with the court was not.*

✦ ✦ ✦

Why I Wrote This Book

Every week, I meet clients who arrive in my office overwhelmed, misinformed, or dangerously underprepared. They have absorbed bad advice from well-meaning friends, outdated assumptions from the internet, or destructive myths about what divorce courts actually do. Some have already made costly mistakes—angry texts they can-not take back, social media posts now preserved as exhibits, financial decisions driven by panic instead of strategy.

And nearly all of them share the same look: the look of someone facing the most consequential legal event of their life without under-standing the rules of the game they are playing.

This book exists to close that gap.

I did not write this to market my law practice. I am not trying to attract local clients. I wrote this because after four decades of watching good people make avoidable mistakes—mistakes that cost them custody time, retirement savings, homes, credibility, and sometimes their relationship with their own children—I de-cided that the knowledge I carry should not stay locked inside my office.

This is a legacy project. It is my attempt to hand you everything I have learned at the front lines, distilled into language you can use immediately, whether your divorce is simple, complex, or violently high-conflict.

> **Core Principle:** *Calm, documented truth wins cases. Panic, anger, and assumptions lose them.*

What This Book Is

This is a field guide for the divorce client. Not a textbook. Not a legal treatise. Not a self-help book filled with platitudes about "finding your truth."

It is a practical, strategic, courtroom-tested manual designed to make you the most prepared, most credible, most effective client your attorney has ever worked with. And if you are navigating this process without an attorney, it will be the closest thing to having one sit across the table and tell you what you actually need to hear.

You will learn how the divorce process works from filing to final judgment. You will understand how judges actually make decisions about property, support, and custody—not how you imagine they make decisions, but how they really do. You will learn what evidence matters and what courts dismiss. You will see how to communicate with your spouse, your attorney, and the court without destroying your credibility. You will learn how to protect your children, your finances, and your emotional stability through a process designed to test all three.

You will also receive scripts you can use verbatim in high-pressure moments, templates for documenting evidence and tracking violations, checklists for every major stage, and sample courtroom testimony that shows you exactly how to present yourself under oath.

This book covers the full spectrum. If your divorce is straightforward and amicable, the financial and procedural chapters will save you from mistakes you did not know you were about to make. If your divorce is complex—involving business valuations, retirement divisions, or hidden assets—the property and discovery chapters will arm you with the knowledge to protect what you have built. And if your divorce is high-conflict, involving a narcissist, an addict, a domestic abuser, or a spouse who uses litigation itself as a weapon, this book will teach you how to survive without becoming what you are fighting.

✦ ✦ ✦

What This Book Is Not

This book is not legal advice. I am licensed to practice law in Louisiana, the District of Columbia, and the State of New York. I am not your attorney. Nothing in these pages tells you what motions to file, what settlement to accept, how your specific judge will rule, or what your case is worth. Every state has different laws. Every case has different facts. Every courthouse has its own culture.

Your attorney's guidance—if you have one—always takes precedence over anything written here.

This book is also not a weapon. You will not find instructions on how to fight dirty, manipulate the system, hide assets, coach witnesses, or destroy your spouse. The strategies here are built on integrity, documentation, and calm credibility—because those are the qualities that win in courtrooms run by experienced judges who have seen every trick imaginable.

And this book is not a promise. No book, no attorney, and no strategy can guarantee an outcome. What I can promise is that if you absorb what is here and apply it with discipline, you will be substantially better prepared than the vast majority of people who walk into a divorce proceeding. In family law, preparation is the closest thing to an advantage that exists.

The Three Things You Control

Divorce strips away your sense of control. You cannot control your spouse's behavior, your attorney's availability, the judge's calendar, the cost of litigation, or the pace of the system. You cannot control whether your spouse lies, hides money, manipulates your children, or weaponizes the process.

But you can control three things—and they are the three things that matter most:

Your clarity. How well you understand the process, the law, and the facts of your own case.

Your credibility. How judges, evaluators, and professionals perceive your honesty, your consistency, and your composure.

Your commitment. Your willingness to prioritize your children's stability and your own future above your anger, your fear, and your desire for revenge.

Strong cases are not built on rage. They are built on documentation, consistency, emotional discipline, and the quiet, persistent presentation of truth. This book is designed to help you build that kind of case.

> **Core Principle:** *Your stability is evidence. Protect it like your case depends on it—because it does.*

THE FOUR PILLARS OF WINNING DIVORCE

The System That Runs Through Every Chapter of This Book

The three things you control—clarity, credibility, and commitment—are the starting point. What follows is the complete system for turning that control into results.

Over nearly four decades and thousands of cases, I have watched the same four factors determine outcomes regardless of the state, the judge, the law firm, or the dollar amount at stake. Clients who build strength in all four factors win. Clients who neglect any one of them pay for it. Every chapter in this book maps to one or more of these pillars. When you understand them, the rest of the book organizes itself.

PILLAR 1: STABILITY

How courts read it: "This parent is reliable. This spouse is steady. The children will be safe here."

Predictable routines. Consistent school involvement. Safe, organized housing. Calm exchanges. Adult boundaries maintained in front of children. Sobriety and compliance with every court order. Stability is the single most powerful message you can send to a judge without saying a word.

Stability is not just parenting. It is courtroom credibility made visible.

PILLAR 2: CREDIBILITY

How courts read it: "This person tells the truth, even when it hurts."

Honesty under pressure. Consistency between what you say, what you write, and what the evidence shows. Composure on the witness stand. Willingness to acknowledge your own mistakes. Credibility is destroyed by exaggeration, contradiction, emotional outbursts, unsupported allegations, and social media theatrics. Once lost, it is nearly impossible to rebuild.

A divorce case is a credibility contest disguised as a legal proceeding.

PILLAR 3: DOCUMENTATION

How courts read it: "This is not drama. This is evidence."

Financial records organized and current. Incident logs maintained contemporaneously. Communications preserved with timestamps and context. Third-party records—school, medical, professional—collected and indexed. Photographs with metadata intact. Every claim supported by something more substantial than your recollection.

Memory is weak. Documentation is durable. Courts trust records.

PILLAR 4: DISCIPLINE

How courts read it: "This person can follow orders and regulate their behavior under stress."

BIFF communication. No retaliation. No court order violations. No impulsive spending, social media posts, or confrontations. Every major decision made through your attorney, not through your anger. Emotional regulation sustained over months and years—not performed for a single hearing.

Discipline under provocation is the rarest form of power in family court.

Every chapter in this book strengthens one or more of these pillars. Every composite case example illustrates what happens when they are present—and what happens when they are missing. When you face a decision during your divorce and are unsure what to do, ask yourself: Does this action strengthen or weaken my Stability, Credibility, Documentation, and Discipline? If it weakens any one of them, stop.

✦ ✦ ✦

THE EVIDENCE LADDER

How Judges Weigh What You Present

Not all evidence carries equal weight. Judges evaluate information along a hierarchy—from the most reliable to the least. The higher your evidence sits on this ladder, the stronger your case. The lower it sits, the more support it needs from the levels above.

Level 1: Verified Records. Bank statements, tax returns, medical records, school reports, police reports, GPS metadata, pay stubs. Independent, verifiable, and nearly impossible to dispute.

Level 2: Neutral Third Parties. Teachers, doctors, therapists, coaches, daycare providers, neighbors who observed specific events. Their testimony carries weight because they have no stake in the outcome.

Level 3: Contemporaneous Documentation. Incident logs written at the time of the event, calendars, screenshots captured with timestamps. Valuable because they were created when the events were fresh—not reconstructed later from memory.

Level 4: Direct Communications. Text messages, emails, voicemails between the parties. Powerful when curated with full context, timestamps, and thread continuity. Dangerous when cherry-picked or taken out of context.

Level 5: Testimony Alone. Your word against theirs. The weakest form of evidence when unsupported by anything higher on the ladder. But when your testimony aligns with Levels 1 through 4, it becomes the voice that connects the evidence into a story the court believes.

The principle: The more your claim depends on testimony alone, the weaker it is. The more it is supported by verified records and neutral witnesses, the stronger it becomes. Build from the top of the ladder down.

THE DIVORCE STRATEGY SCORECARD

Rate yourself honestly. Revisit monthly.

Before you read further, take sixty seconds to assess where you stand right now. Rate yourself 1 (not at all) through 5 (exceptionally strong) in each pillar:

Stability _________ / 5

Credibility _________ / 5

Documentation _________ / 5

Discipline _________ / 5

TOTAL: _________ / 20

16–20: Strategically strong. You are positioned well. This book will sharpen what you are already doing right.

12–15: Vulnerable but fixable. You have gaps that opposing counsel will find. This book will show you where they are and how to close them.

8–11: High risk of self-inflicted damage. Your case is at risk—not from your spouse's strength but from your own vulnerabilities. Read carefully. Apply immediately.

Below 8: Stop and stabilize. Turn to the 72-Hour Triage Guide on page [XX] right now. Address the crisis before attempting strategy.

> Retake this scorecard every month. Your score should improve as you apply the guidance in each chapter. If it does not, reread the chapters that address your weakest pillar.
>
> **Core Principle:** *Four pillars. One system. Every chapter in this book strengthens at least one. Every mistake you avoid protects all four. This is how cases are won—not with a single dramatic moment, but with sustained, disciplined strength across every dimension the court evaluates.*

THE THREE PHASES OF DIVORCE STRATEGY

Phase 1: Stabilize

Stop the bleeding. Prevent catastrophic early mistakes. Secure your safety, your finances, and your children's routines. Lock down communications. Begin documentation. Assemble your professional team.

Reader promise: In 72 hours, you will stop the panic and start the plan.

Covered in: Introduction, 72-Hour Triage, Parts I, II, and VII

Phase 2: Build

Strengthen your position through evidence, financial clarity, and professional preparation. Complete discovery. Organize your exhibits. Develop your parenting plan. Coordinate your legal, financial, and therapeutic team. This phase is where leverage is constructed—not through argument, but through meticulous preparation.

Reader promise: You do not argue your way into leverage. You build it.

Covered in: Parts III, IV, V, VI, VIII, and XI–XII

◆ ◆ ◆

Phase 3: Resolve

Settle wisely or try the case cleanly. Enter mediation prepared. Take the stand with composure and specificity. Enforce the decree. Rebuild your life and your family's stability beyond the courthouse.

Reader promise: The goal is not court. The goal is a durable life.

Covered in: Parts IX, X, and XI–XII

> **Core Principle:** *These three phases are not rigid stages—you may cycle between them as your case develops. But the sequence matters: stabilize before you build, and build before you try to resolve. Clients who skip Phase 1 undermine everything that follows.*

HOW TO USE THIS BOOK

Especially If You Are Already in a Live Case

If you are holding this book, your world may already feel as though it is tilting on its axis. You may be exhausted, overwhelmed, terrified, furious, or operating on nothing but adrenaline and coffee. Divorce does that. It demands enormous decisions at the precise moment your nervous system feels least equipped to make them.

So before you turn another page, take one breath. You are here. You are seeking clarity instead of flailing in the dark. That decision alone puts you ahead of most people who walk into this process unprepared.

This book is designed to be used during the storm—not after it passes. You do not need to read it cover to cover before it helps you. You do not need a law degree or any prior legal knowledge. You simply need the willingness to prepare instead of panic.

> **Core Principle:** *Use this book your way. There is no wrong entry point.*

1. Start Where the Fire Is Burning

You may want to read every chapter in order. You do not have to. If something is urgent—a hearing next week, a hostile text thread, a discovery deadline, a financial emergency, a safety concern—go directly to the chapter that addresses that crisis. This book is built so you can enter anywhere and find guidance that applies immediately.

IF YOU'RE DEALING WITH…

An immediate crisis or emergency → Your Divorce Triage: The First 72 Hours (this section, next chapter)

Property division concerns or hidden assets → Part VI, Chapters 20–24

Spousal support or alimony questions → Part V, Chapters 17–19

Child support or expense disputes → Part IV, Chapters 14–16

Custody fundamentals → Part III, Chapters 10–13 (plus the companion volume for deep coverage)

Domestic violence or a safety threat → Chapter 25

Restraining orders or injunctions → Chapter 26

Substance abuse (yours or your spouse's) → Chapter 27

A narcissist or high-conflict personality → Chapter 4 and Chapter 28

Parental alienation → Chapter 29 (plus companion book Chapter 12)

Finding or working with a lawyer → Chapter 30

Mediation preparation → Chapter 33

A hearing or trial approaching → Part IX, Chapters 35–37

Social media exposure or digital evidence → Chapter 9

Representing yourself → Chapter 34

2. Read in Short Bursts

Stress and trauma disrupt memory, concentration, and decision-making. If you read a paragraph and immediately forget what it said, that is not a failure of intelligence—it is a predictable effect of what your nervous system is processing. Work with that reality, not against it. Read one section at a time. Underline or highlight what strikes you. Return to the same page as many times as you need. This book is meant to be picked up, put down, and returned to throughout your case.

3. Skip Ahead When You Have a Deadline

If mediation is scheduled for next Tuesday, turn to Chapter 33 now. If you have a hearing in three days, go to Chapter 35. If your attorney asked you to organize financial documents, open Chapter 47 and use the templates. This book contains scripts, checklists, and preparation guides designed to be used the same day you read them. Treat it as a real-time field manual, not a homework assignment.

4. Use the Scripts and Templates Before You Trust Your Own Words

In divorce, wording matters. Tone matters. What you put in writing becomes permanent evidence. The scripts in Part XII have been refined across thousands of cases to keep you calm, prevent self-sabotage, and demonstrate the maturity courts reward. When emotion is running high and you are tempted to fire off a response, open this book instead. Use the language exactly as written. Once you feel steady, adapt the wording to sound like you—but when in doubt, the scripts are safer than your instincts.

5. Do Not Skip the Mindset Chapters

You may be tempted to jump straight to the legal strategy and skip the chapters on emotional regulation, communication discipline, and mental health. That would be a mistake. In my experience, cases are lost far more often because a client sent a reckless text, melted down in front of an evaluator, or made a financial decision driven by revenge than because their attorney made a legal error. Your emotional steadiness is one of the most powerful forms of evidence you will ever present. Protect it.

6. Use This Book Even If You Have a Lawyer

Your attorney handles the legal strategy, the filings, and the courtroom advocacy. Your attorney cannot, however, follow you home. A lawyer cannot stop you from responding to a provocative text at midnight, posting something emotional on social media, confronting your spouse about a discovered affair, or making a financial decision in the heat of the moment. You carry the bulk of the daily conduct that shapes how judges, evaluators, and professionals perceive you. This book teaches you how to become the kind of client who strengthens your attorney's work instead of undermining it.

7. Use This Book Even If You Have No Lawyer

If you are representing yourself or using limited-scope legal services, this book becomes your roadmap, your translator, your strategy guide, and your communication coach. You will learn how to stay organized, how to speak to the court, how to document your concerns, and how to avoid the procedural mistakes that self-represented litigants make most often. You are not alone in this process just because you do not have full-time counsel.

8. Return to the Checklists Relentlessly

The checklists in the appendices are designed for repeated use: before filing, before mediation, before a hearing, before a deposition, and after judgment. When stress makes your mind go blank—and it will—these lists remember what you cannot. Photocopy them. Dog-ear the pages. Keep them on your nightstand. They are among the most practical tools in this book.

9. Use This Book to Reclaim Your Power

Divorce strips power away from people. This book is designed to return it—not through aggression, manipulation, or retaliation, but through knowledge, preparation, and calm strength. The more you understand the process, the less frightened you feel. The less frightened you feel, the better decisions you make. The better your decisions, the more protected your children, your finances, and your future become. That is how this book serves you.

10. Use This Book with Hope

Your divorce may be difficult, but it is not hopeless. You may feel exhausted, but you are not broken. You may feel lost, but credible guidance is now in your hands. The insight gathered across these pages comes from thousands of cases, decades in courtrooms, and a career devoted to protecting families during their most vulnerable chapters.

Use this book with intention. Use it with discipline. And use it with the understanding that preparation is the single greatest advantage any divorce client can possess.

Your children need you steady. Your future needs you strategic. And your case needs you prepared.

WHAT I ASK OF YOU

Five Commitments Before You Begin

Before you move into the strategies, templates, and legal education that fill these pages, I need to ask something of you. Not as your attorney—I am not. But as someone who has walked thousands of clients through this process and has learned what separates those who protect their families from those who unintentionally destroy their own cases.

These five commitments will determine whether this book transforms your preparation or simply collects dust. Make them now.

1. Read with an Open Mind

Some of what you read here will feel counterintuitive. You may believe your situation is different, that the rules do not apply to your case, that your spouse is uniquely terrible and therefore the usual strategies will not work. Read anyway. The guidance in this book comes from watching what succeeds and what fails across thousands of cases over nearly four decades. Trust the process, especially when it contradicts your instincts.

2. Use the Tools Provided

This book contains scripts, templates, checklists, and communication strategies refined over decades of practice. They are here because they work. When you are triggered, panicked, or unsure what to say, open this book and follow the guidance as written. Do not improvise when the stakes are this high. The tools exist to keep you out of trouble and to demonstrate the discipline that judges reward.

3. Stay Focused on Your Children and Your Future

Every decision you make—every text you send, every dollar you spend, every word you speak in court—must pass one test: does this protect my children's well-being and serve my long-term interests? Not your ego. Not your anger. Not your need to punish your spouse or prove you were right. Your children and your future. When you lose sight of that compass, you lose ground in your case.

4. Seek Professional Help

This book does not replace a lawyer, a therapist, a financial advisor, or a substance abuse counselor. It is a guide designed to help you work more effectively with those professionals. Divorce—especially contested divorce—is too complex, too consequential, and too emotionally demanding to navigate without a team. Strength is not doing everything alone. Strength is assembling the right support and using it wisely.

5. Give Yourself Grace

You will make mistakes. You will react emotionally when you meant to stay calm. You will send a message you regret, miss a detail, or feel certain that you are failing. None of that disqualifies you. What matters is that you recognize the misstep, correct course, and keep moving forward with honesty and intention. The standard is not perfection. The standard is consistency, self-awareness, and the willingness to learn.

6. Be Financially Honest with Yourself

This commitment is specific to divorce, and it is one most clients resist. You must understand your true financial picture—what you own, what you owe, what you earn, and what your life actually costs—before you can protect anything. Clients who refuse to confront financial realities make the most expensive mistakes in family law. Denial about money is not a defense; it is a vulnerability.

If you can commit to these six principles, you are ready. This book will meet you wherever you are and help you become the client who walks into every meeting, every mediation session, and every courtroom prepared, credible, and impossible to underestimate.

WHAT THIS BOOK WILL
AND WILL NOT DO

What This Book Will Do

1. Give you a clear, grounded understanding of the divorce process. You will learn how divorce works from the moment a petition is filed through final judgment and beyond—including temporary orders, discovery, mediation, settlement negotiations, and trial. You will understand timelines, procedures, and the decisions that must be made at each stage.

2. Teach you how judges actually decide cases. Judges do not rule based on who cries harder or tells the more sympathetic story. They rely on statutory factors, credibility assessments, financial evidence, behavioral patterns, and the best interests of children. This book translates those criteria into plain language so you can make choices that align with what courts actually value.

3. Show you how to communicate in ways that protect your case. You will learn how to respond to hostile messages, what never to put in writing, how to speak in court and mediation, and how to avoid the communication mistakes that destroy credibility faster than any legal maneuver. Every text, email, and statement you make is a potential exhibit. This book teaches you to communicate as if a judge is reading over your shoulder.

4. Arm you with tools to document properly and powerfully. Courts routinely ignore emotional narratives and reward organized, factual evidence. You will learn how to gather, organize, and present documentation that judges trust, with templates and checklists you can begin using immediately.

5. Protect your children emotionally and psychologically. This book goes well beyond legal strategy. You will learn how to shield children from parental conflict, recognize signs of distress, respond when your spouse pulls them into the fight, and support their stability through a process that is inherently destabilizing. Your children's well-being sits at the center of everything in these pages.

6. Help you work effectively with every professional who touches your case. Lawyers, financial advisors, forensic accountants, therapists, custody evaluators, and mediators all influence your outcome. You will learn how to choose the right professionals, communicate with them efficiently, control costs, and present yourself in a way that earns their respect and trust.

7. Prepare you for every major moment. Whether you are facing mediation, a deposition, a temporary hearing, or a full trial, you will know what to expect, how to prepare, and how to present yourself with the composure and credibility that judges reward.

8. Provide scripts, templates, and tools you can deploy the same day you read them. Part XII of this book delivers communication scripts, evidence templates, financial worksheets, courtroom Q&A examples, and checklists for every major stage. These are not theoretical—they are field-tested instruments designed for real-world pressure.

9. Strengthen your emotional resilience. Divorce is a marathon fought at sprint intensity. This book will help you regulate your emotions, reduce reactivity, maintain clarity under sustained pressure, and avoid the impulsive mistakes that exhausted, frightened people make. Over time, you will become steadier, sharper, and more strategic.

10. Make you the client every good attorney wants to represent. Every chapter is engineered to help you demonstrate what courts value most: preparation, maturity, stability, honesty, and a genuine commitment to your children's well-being and your own future. When you show up with those qualities, you become formidable.

What This Book Will Not Do

1. This book will not give you legal advice. Every state has its own laws, every case has its own facts, and every judge has a distinct approach to the bench. This book cannot tell you what to file, what to accept, or how your judge will rule. Only a licensed attorney in your jurisdiction can provide that guidance.

2. This book will not replace your lawyer. Even the most prepared client still needs counsel for legal strategy, procedural requirements, and courtroom advocacy. This book makes you a better partner to your attorney, not a substitute for one.

3. This book will not diagnose anyone. You will read about narcissistic patterns, addictive behaviors, coercive control, and other dynamics common in contested divorce. This book describes behaviors to help you recognize and respond to them. It does not diagnose your spouse or you. Only licensed professionals can do that.

4. This book will not promise you a win. No book, attorney, expert, or strategy can guarantee any outcome. What this book can do is substantially improve your preparation, your credibility, and your decision-making—which are the factors most closely correlated with favorable results.

5. This book will not encourage escalation. You will find no instructions for retaliation, manipulation, or aggression. This book is about protection and strategic strength, not destruction.

6. This book will not endorse using children as leverage. It will not support coaching children, using them as messengers, interrogating them about the other parent, or forming alliances against your spouse through your kids. Children deserve protection from the conflict, not a role in it.

7. This book will not pretend you can do this alone. Throughout these pages, you will be encouraged to engage attorneys, therapists, financial professionals, and other experts. Divorce is too consequential to navigate without support.

8. This book will not shame you. You may have made mistakes. You may have stayed too long, reacted poorly, missed warning signs, or handled money badly. This book is about what happens next—not about punishing you for what came before.

> **Core Principle:** *This book educates. It does not advise. But the education it provides can fundamentally change the trajectory of your case.*

THE 10 DIVORCE RULES YOU MUST NEVER BREAK

Unbreakable principles that protect your case, your children, and your credibility

These ten rules form the structural backbone of every successful divorce strategy I have observed across nearly four decades of practice. I have watched clients follow them and prevail in cases that seemed unwinnable. I have watched other clients break them and lose cases that should have been straightforward.

They are deceptively simple. Following them when you are calm is easy. Following them at two in the morning when your spouse has just sent a message designed to detonate your composure—that is where discipline separates the clients who protect their cases from the clients who destroy them.

Read these rules carefully. Return to them often. Tape them to your bathroom mirror if you must. They are here to save you from the most expensive, most damaging, and most common mistakes clients make.

Core Principle: *Your behavior is always evidence. Every action you take either strengthens or weakens your case. There are no neutral moves in divorce.*

Rule 1: Never Put Anything in Writing You Would Not Want a Judge to Read Aloud in Open Court

Every text message, email, direct message, voicemail, social media comment, and handwritten note you produce during your divorce is a potential courtroom exhibit. Before you hit send on anything, imagine the judge reading those exact words from the bench while your attorney sits beside you. If that image makes your stomach drop, do not send it. Self-control in written communication is not weakness. It is one of the most powerful forms of evidence a client can produce.

WHAT I'VE SEEN: The Text That Became Exhibit A

At 11:47 PM on a Tuesday, Greg received a message from his ex-wife claiming he had forgotten their daughter's dentist appointment—an appointment that had been rescheduled without his knowledge. Exhausted and furious, Greg fired back: 'You are a manipulative, lying piece of work. You deliberately kept me in the dark so you could make me look bad. I am DONE playing nice. You want a war? You've got one.' That message was printed, enlarged to poster size, and presented as the opening exhibit at his temporary custody hearing six weeks later. Opposing counsel read it aloud while Greg sat unable to make eye contact with the judge. Had Greg waited thirty minutes and sent a BIFF response—'I wasn't notified of the schedule change. Please confirm the new date so I can update my calendar'—the hearing would have focused on the mother's failure to communicate, not on his inability to control his temper. One text. Eleven seconds to type. Eighteen months of credibility damage.

Rule 2: Do Not Involve Your Children in the Conflict—in Any Form, for Any Reason

Do not vent to your child. Do not ask them to deliver messages. Do not interrogate them about the other parent's home, dating life, finances, or behavior. Do not criticize your spouse in their presence—even if you believe they cannot hear you. Do not use your children as emotional support, allies, or intelligence sources. Courts identify and punish parents who draw children into adult conflict, and they protect parents who demonstrably shield children from it. Your child is not your confidant. Your child is the reason you are fighting.

Rule 3: Never Respond When You Are Angry, Panicked, or Emotionally Flooded

High-conflict spouses are often gifted at provocation. They know exactly what to say, when to say it, and how to phrase it to trigger an emotional reaction they can then screenshot and hand to their attorney. Your rule is straightforward: do not respond from adrenaline. Wait. Breathe. Open this book. Use the scripts in Part XII. Respond only when you are calm, factual, and deliberate. Reactive communication is the single most common way good clients damage good cases.

Rule 4: Do Not Post About Your Case or Your Spouse on Social Media

No rants. No vague inspirational quotes that are clearly directed at your spouse. No subtweets. No photographs of your new car, new partner, new vacation, or new lifestyle while claiming you cannot afford support. No "cryptic" messages your friends will immediately decode. Social media content is routinely admitted as evidence in divorce proceedings, and it destroys credibility with startling efficiency. If you would not want a judge to see it, do not post it.

Rule 5: Always Assume You Are Being Recorded, Monitored, and Scrutinized

In contested divorce—especially high-conflict cases—assume everything you say, text, post, and do may be observed, recorded, or reported. Speak as though the courtroom microphone is always on. Behave at exchanges as though a video camera is running—because it may well be. This is not paranoia. It is the operational reality of modern family law litigation.

✦ ✦ ✦

Rule 6: Do Not Make Allegations You Cannot Substantiate

Judges encounter false and exaggerated claims constantly, and they develop a sharp instinct for distinguishing genuine concerns from tactical accusations. An allegation you cannot support with evidence does not damage your spouse—it damages you. Raise concerns only when you have documentation, witnesses, records, or other credible support. This book will teach you how to build that support properly.

✦ ✦ ✦

Rule 7: Do Not Violate Court Orders—Even When Your Spouse Violates Them First

This is where otherwise intelligent clients make catastrophic mistakes. Your spouse fails to return the children on time, so you withhold them the following week. Your spouse stops paying support, so you deny visitation. Your spouse violates the communication protocols, so you respond in kind. Every one of these reactions hands your spouse's attorney a gift. Judges do not accept "they did it first" as a defense. Follow every order to the letter. When your spouse violates an order, document it meticulously and address it through proper legal channels. Courts often punish the retaliator more harshly than the initial violator.

Rule 8: Do Not Hide, Dissipate, Transfer, or Destroy Marital Assets

Moving money into a relative's account. Transferring property to a friend. Running personal expenses through a business. Making "gifts" to a new partner. Liquidating retirement accounts without disclosure. These are not clever strategies—they are actionable offenses that courts penalize through adverse findings, unequal distribution, sanctions, and in some cases, criminal referral. Full financial transparency is not optional in divorce. It is mandatory.

Rule 9: Protect Your Mental Health— Deliberately and Visibly

Judges, evaluators, and professionals observe your emotional state throughout the process. A parent who engages in therapy, manages stress constructively, and demonstrates self-awareness earns credibility. A parent who denies needing help, self-medicates, or displays volatile emotional swings raises concerns. Protecting your mental health is not an indulgence during divorce—it is a strategic imperative.

Rule 10: Never Pursue Victory Through Harm

Do not withhold children without legal basis. Do not interfere with parenting time. Do not destroy property, stalk your spouse, harass their new partner, create fabricated evidence, recruit your children as allies, or use intimidation. These actions almost always produce consequences far worse than any short-term satisfaction they deliver.

You do not win a divorce by causing damage. You win by being prepared, credible, consistent, and relentlessly focused on what serves your children and your future.

The Foundation

These ten rules are simple to understand and extraordinarily difficult to follow when your world is burning. Your spouse may provoke you deliberately, knowing that your reaction will become their evidence. Friends and family may encourage you to "fight back" in ways that feel satisfying but are legally destructive. Your own pain may whisper that the rules do not apply because your situation is different.

The rules always apply. They apply to simple divorces and nuclear ones. They apply when you are right and when you are wronged. They apply at two in the afternoon and at two in the morning.

Treat them as the foundation beneath your feet. They will protect your credibility, your stability, your children, and your future—if you let them.

Core Principle: *Discipline under pressure is the rarest and most valuable quality a divorce client can demonstrate. These ten rules are how you prove you have it.*

YOUR DIVORCE TRIAGE
The First 72 Hours of Clarity

When divorce becomes real—whether you filed or were served, whether it escalated overnight or had been building for years—the first seventy-two hours establish a trajectory that can persist for the remainder of the case. This is the window when panic runs highest, mistakes are most frequent, and a single impulsive decision can inflict damage that takes months or years to repair.

You do not need to execute everything perfectly. You simply need to follow this sequence, avoid the most common traps, and begin the shift from emotional reaction to strategic action. That shift is what separates clients who protect their families from clients who inadvertently harm their own position.

> **Core Principle:** *In crisis, slow down and follow the plan. Speed feels necessary. Discipline actually is.*

✦ ✦ ✦

HOUR 0 – 1: STOP THE BLEEDING

Freeze all emotional communication. If your spouse has just served you, confronted you, sent hostile messages, or dropped a bombshell, do not respond from emotion. Do not defend yourself via text. Do not call to argue. Do not fire off a lengthy email explaining how unfair this is. A single reactive message sent in the first hour can become the opposing attorney's favorite exhibit for the next eighteen months. Your immediate rule: respond only when calm, using the communication scripts in this book.

Complete social media blackout. Not even vague posts, uplifting quotes, or "cryptic" messages your friends will decode. Screenshots are forever. Judges see them routinely. Log out of every platform and do not return until your attorney clears you—or until the case is resolved.

Shield your children. Do not discuss the divorce, the filing, or your spouse's behavior with your children. Do not cry, vent, or argue within their hearing. Do not ask them questions about the other parent. Protecting your child's emotional environment in this first hour is the single most important action you can take.

Secure critical documents. Locate and copy—do not remove originals—birth certificates, marriage certificate, recent tax returns, bank and investment account statements, mortgage documents, insurance policies, vehicle titles, and any existing court orders. Store copies in a secure location outside the marital home—a trusted friend's house, a safe deposit box, or a secure cloud account your spouse cannot access.

Note financial account balances. Log into every joint and individual bank account, credit card, retirement account, and investment account you can access. Screenshot or print the current balances. This establishes a baseline. Do not move, withdraw, or transfer money without first consulting an attorney.

Do NOT leave the marital home without legal advice. Unless you are in physical danger, do not vacate the residence before speaking with an attorney. Leaving can affect your claims to the property and your position in custody. If you are in danger, leave immediately and contact law enforcement or the National Domestic Violence Hotline at 1-800-799-7233.

HOUR 1 – 6: SECURE YOUR FOUNDATION

Begin gathering financial documentation. Three years of tax returns. Six months of bank statements for every account. Recent pay stubs or proof of income for both spouses. Credit card statements. Mortgage and loan documents. Retirement and investment account statements. Business records if either spouse is self-employed. You do not need everything today—but start building the financial picture now. The clients who organize their finances early gain an advantage that compounds throughout the case.

Start your incident and communication log. Using the template provided in Part XII of this book, begin recording events as they happen: date, time, what occurred, who was present, and how it affected your children. Record facts only—not interpretations, not emotions, not commentary. Courts trust contemporaneous records far more than memories reconstructed weeks or months later.

Consult with an attorney. If you already have counsel, send a brief, organized summary of what has happened—facts only, essential documents attached. If you do not have an attorney, begin calling offices today. Ask the questions outlined in Chapter 30 of this book. Understand that your first consultation is about evaluating the lawyer as much as it is about evaluating your case.

Assess immediate safety concerns. Ask yourself directly: is there domestic violence, substance abuse, serious mental instability, or any situation where you or your children are in danger? If the answer is yes, follow the safety protocols in Chapters 25 and 26. Safety takes precedence over every other consideration—but it can be addressed alongside strategic preparation.

HOUR 6 – 24: STABILIZE

Shift all communication to the BIFF framework. From this moment forward, every message to your spouse should be Brief, Informative, Friendly (or at minimum neutral), and Firm. This communication style prevents escalation and creates a written record that presents you as measured, child-focused, and cooperative. You will find detailed BIFF guidance and examples throughout this book.

Establish safe, predictable routines for your children. Maintain regular mealtimes, bedtimes, school schedules, and extracurricular activities as closely as possible. Stability in your child's daily experience is powerful evidence of attentive parenting—and it is the right thing to do regardless of the legal context.

Assess risk factors. Consider whether your situation involves domestic violence, hidden or dissipating assets, flight risk, substance abuse, or parental alienation. Each of these requires specific, targeted responses addressed in dedicated chapters of this book.

Begin your personal stabilization plan. Schedule a therapy appointment if possible. Prioritize sleep, nutrition, and exercise—your physical health directly affects your cognitive function and emotional regulation. Reduce exposure to people and situations that escalate your distress. Judges consistently favor parents who demonstrate the self-awareness to seek appropriate support.

HOUR 24 – 72: BUILD YOUR FRAMEWORK

Organize your evidence. Begin assembling a working case binder—physical or digital—organized chronologically. Include your incident log, financial documents, saved communications, and any police reports, medical records, or school records that are relevant. The template in Chapter 47 will guide the structure.

Begin your financial inventory. Start listing every asset you know about (real estate, vehicles, bank accounts, retirement accounts, investments, valuables), every debt (mortgages, loans, credit cards, tax obligations), and every source of income for both you and your spouse. You will refine this inventory over time, but the initial sketch should begin now.

Identify potential witnesses. Consider who has observed relevant facts: friends, family members, neighbors, teachers, coaches, counselors, doctors, coworkers, daycare providers. Note their names and what they may be able to corroborate. Your attorney will help prioritize and prepare this list later.

Create your Case Clarity Summary. Draft a one-page document that outlines: your primary concerns, your strengths as a parent and spouse, the evidence you currently have, and what you are asking the court to do. Lawyers value this enormously. It demonstrates organization, self-awareness, and strategic thinking—and it focuses your early meetings on substance rather than venting.

Understand the status quo. The living arrangements, financial patterns, and parenting routines that exist during the first weeks of separation often become the baseline against which a court measures future requests. Be intentional about what patterns you are establishing. Consult your attorney about temporary orders that may be available to formalize the status quo in your favor.

WHAT NOT TO DO IN THE FIRST 72 HOURS

- Do not confront your spouse about discovered infidelity, hidden accounts, or lies. Document first; address through counsel.
- Do not move money, close accounts, or change beneficiaries without legal advice.

- Do not change the locks on the marital home without legal advice.

- Do not introduce your children to a new romantic partner.

- Do not record conversations without confirming your state's recording laws with an attorney.

- Do not destroy any documents, devices, photographs, or potential evidence—yours or your spouse's.

- Do not sign any agreement, settlement proposal, or legal document without your attorney's review.

- Do not make major financial decisions—purchasing a car, leasing an apartment, taking on debt—without consulting counsel.

- Do not disparage your spouse to mutual friends, family members, or—most critically—your children.

Shifting from Reaction to Strategy

By the end of seventy-two hours, your goal is not to have solved everything. It is to have stabilized your immediate situation, secured your critical documents, begun the documentation habit, engaged or identified legal counsel, protected your children from the crossfire, and taken the first deliberate steps from survival mode into strategic positioning.

You do not need to be flawless. You do not need to have every answer. You need to be moving in the right direction with the right information—and that is precisely what this book will continue to provide, chapter by chapter, through every stage of the process ahead.

> **Core Principle:** *The decisions you make in the first 72 hours echo throughout the entire case. Make them from clarity, not chaos.*

Every pillar begins here. These chapters establish the knowledge base that prevents catastrophic early mistakes.

PART I

UNDERSTANDING DIVORCE: WHAT YOU ARE FACING

CHAPTER 1

The Anatomy of Divorce — Simple, Complex, and High-Conflict

Most people enter divorce imagining a single version of the process—one shaped by movies, internet forums, or the cautionary tale of someone they know. The actual landscape is far more varied, and understanding where your case sits on that landscape is the first strategic decision you will make.

Divorce is not one experience. It is a spectrum. On one end, two reasonable adults agree to part ways and divide their lives with minimal conflict. On the other end, one or both parties wage a legal and emotional war that consumes years, drains bank accounts, traumatizes children, and leaves permanent scars. Most cases fall somewhere in between—and many shift position as circumstances change.

This chapter will help you recognize where your case currently falls, what forces cause cases to escalate, and why understanding the terrain matters before you take a single strategic step.

What Divorce Actually Is

At its core, divorce is the legal dissolution of a civil contract. A marriage is a legal relationship that creates specific rights and obligations under state law—rights to shared property, obligations of mutual support, presumptions of parentage, and a framework for decision-making about children. Divorce terminates that legal relationship and replaces it with a judgment that governs the same issues going forward.

That judgment must resolve, at minimum, the division of property and debts, the question of whether either spouse will pay support to the other, and—if children are involved—custody, visitation, and child support. In simple cases, the parties reach agreement on these issues and present a consent judgment to the court. In contested cases, a judge decides after hearing evidence from both sides.

The emotional dimension of divorce—the grief, the anger, the betrayal, the fear—is real and valid, but it operates on a separate track from the legal process. The court's job is not to determine who was the better spouse, who caused the marriage to fail, or who deserves more sympathy. The court's job is to divide assets equitably, provide appropriate support where the law requires it, and protect children. Understanding this distinction early will save you enormous frustration and help you channel your energy where it actually matters.

The Three Tiers of Divorce

Every divorce I have handled in nearly four decades falls somewhere on a spectrum defined by three general tiers. Recognizing which tier your case occupies—and being alert to the forces that push cases from one tier to the next—is essential to strategic preparation.

Tier 1: Simple or Uncontested Divorce

Both parties agree to end the marriage. They are willing to negotiate the division of assets and debts, can communicate about custody without constant conflict, and share a general desire to resolve things efficiently. Assets may be modest or may simply be straightforward to divide. There are no serious safety concerns, no hidden money, no personality disorders driving the process.

Simple divorces can often be resolved through mediation or direct negotiation, with attorneys reviewing the final agreement. Legal fees are relatively contained. Timelines are shorter. The emotional toll, while still real, is manageable.

The trap in simple divorces is assuming that "simple" means "risk-free." Even amicable dissolutions involve binding legal decisions about property, retirement accounts, support obligations, and parenting schedules that will govern your life for years or decades. Clients who treat simple divorces casually—who sign agreements without full financial disclosure, who forgo attorney review to save a few hundred dollars, or who agree to vague parenting plans to avoid uncomfortable conversations—often find themselves back in court within two years, spending far more than they saved.

WHAT I'VE SEEN: The Simple Divorce That Wasn't

Natalie and James agreed on almost everything. No children. Modest assets. Both employed. They used an online template for their settlement. The template did not address James's 401(k), which held $185,000—the largest single asset in the marriage. It also omitted a QDRO, the specialized order required to divide retirement accounts without triggering penalties and taxes. Natalie signed believing she would receive half as discussed. Two years later, when she attempted to claim her share, she discovered that without a QDRO, she had no legal mechanism to access the funds. James, who had remarried, refused to cooperate. Natalie hired an attorney, filed a motion to reopen the property division, and spent $9,400 in legal fees to obtain what a $500 attorney review at the time of signing would have secured.

Tier 2: Complex Divorce

The parties may or may not be amicable, but the financial or custodial picture is complicated. One or both spouses own a business. There are multiple properties, significant retirement accounts, stock options, or deferred compensation. Income may be disputed—one spouse is self-employed, or one has significantly reduced their earnings since separation. Custody is contested but not yet toxic. There may be disagreements about spousal support, private school, relocation, or the valuation of specific assets.

Complex divorces require professional support beyond a single attorney: forensic accountants, business valuators, real estate appraisers, custody evaluators, vocational experts, or Certified Divorce Financial Analysts. The discovery phase—the legal process of compelling disclosure of financial information—becomes critical. Legal fees are higher and timelines stretch longer.

The challenge in complex cases is the temptation to litigate everything. Not every disputed dollar justifies the cost of fighting over it. Strategic prioritization—understanding which issues deserve maximum resources and which deserve strategic concession—is the skill that separates effective divorce clients from those who win battles but lose wars.

Tier 3: High-Conflict Divorce

High-conflict divorce is a fundamentally different experience. It is defined not by the size of the marital estate or the complexity of the financial picture, but by the behavior of one or both parties.

In high-conflict cases, at least one spouse consistently escalates tension, distorts reality, refuses accountability, and treats the legal process as a battleground rather than a resolution mechanism. High-conflict cases frequently involve narcissistic or personality-disordered behavior, domestic violence or coercive control, substance abuse, parental alienation, false allegations, or the strategic weaponization of the court system itself.

These cases are exhausting, expensive, emotionally devastating, and dangerous to children. They demand comprehensive legal strategy, robust documentation, emotional resilience, and a level of discipline that most people have never been asked to sustain.

The distinctive feature of high-conflict divorce is that conventional approaches—reasoning, compromise, appeals to fairness—do not work. You cannot negotiate rationally with someone who is motivated by control rather than resolution. You cannot mediate effectively with a spouse who views concession as weakness and uses every interaction as an opportunity for manipulation. The strategies required are specific, and they are addressed throughout this book.

WHAT I'VE SEEN: The Case That Changed Tiers Overnight

Marcus and Denise started with what looked like a Tier 2 divorce—a family business to value, two rental properties, and mild disagreement about the parenting schedule. Their attorneys expected settlement within six months. Then Denise's new boyfriend moved into the marital home while custody was pending. Marcus confronted Denise at a school event. Denise filed for a protective order the following Monday—not because Marcus had been violent, but because the order would give her exclusive use of the home and temporary primary custody. Marcus was served at his office in front of coworkers. Humiliated and enraged, he posted a seven-paragraph attack on Facebook naming Denise and her boyfriend. The post was screenshotted within an hour. What had been a negotiable financial dispute became a two-year war involving a custody evaluator, a forensic accountant, a guardian ad litem, and a five-day trial. Combined legal fees exceeded $180,000. The boyfriend was the match. The Facebook post was the accelerant. And the protective order—filed tactically rather than from genuine fear—set the entire case ablaze.

Why Cases Migrate Between Tiers

Cases rarely stay where they start. A divorce that begins as a civil conversation can escalate to high-conflict overnight when one spouse discovers an affair, uncovers hidden assets, or learns that the other parent intends to relocate with the children.

Common escalation triggers include:

- Discovery of infidelity or financial deception
- Introduction of a new romantic partner—especially to the children
- One spouse's refusal to disclose financial information
- Substance abuse relapse or mental health crisis
- Parental alienation behaviors emerging as separation becomes real
- A retaliatory filing: protective orders, abuse allegations, or emergency custody motions
- External pressure from family members, new partners, or social media exposure
- One spouse hiring an aggressive attorney who approaches the case as warfare rather than resolution

The lesson is straightforward: prepare for the case you might have, not only the case you think you have. Clients who assume their divorce will remain simple and prepare accordingly are the most vulnerable when it does not.

The Emotional Stages and Their Impact on Legal Decisions

Divorce activates grief—even when you are the one who initiated it. The emotional trajectory is not linear, and it does not follow a predictable timeline, but certain patterns appear consistently:

Shock and denial in the earliest days, when the reality has not yet settled. Anger and blame as the loss becomes concrete and the legal process begins. Bargaining, where one or both spouses attempt to salvage something—the marriage, the house, the illusion that things can return to what they were. Depression and grief as the permanence sets in. And eventually, acceptance and forward motion.

The critical point for your case is this: each of these emotional states produces a different kind of decision-making, and not all of it is sound. Clients in denial agree to settlements that are wildly unfavorable because they cannot yet accept that the divorce is real. Clients consumed by anger pursue scorched-earth litigation strategies that cost a fortune and produce worse outcomes than negotiation would have. Clients in the bargaining phase make irrational concessions to keep the peace or to punish themselves for perceived failures. Clients in depression stop engaging with their case entirely, missing deadlines and ignoring attorney communications.

The rule is simple: do not make permanent legal decisions from temporary emotional states.

If you are in the early weeks of your divorce and your emotions are volatile—and they almost certainly are—this is the single most important sentence in this chapter. Write it down. Tape it to your refrigerator. Tell your attorney to remind you of it before you approve any major decision.

The Gap Between What You Feel and What the Court Sees

One of the most disorienting aspects of divorce is the disconnect between your emotional experience and the court's assessment of your case. You know your spouse lied. You know they were unfaithful. You know they are a terrible parent, or a manipulative person, or a financial predator. You have lived it.

The court does not know any of that. The court knows only what is presented to it through admissible evidence, credible testimony, and organized documentation. A judge who has fifteen minutes to review your temporary hearing cannot absorb twenty years of marital history. A judge making a custody determination evaluates specific factors defined by statute—not the entire emotional narrative of your relationship.

This gap is where cases are won and lost. Clients who learn to translate their lived experience into the language the court understands—organized evidence, calm testimony, credible documentation—prevail. Clients who assume the court will somehow perceive the full picture without that translation are routinely disappointed.

Closing that gap is precisely what this book is designed to help you do.

Core Principle: *Your divorce is not your identity. It is a legal process that demands strategic navigation regardless of how it makes you feel. The clients who understand this early gain an advantage that compounds throughout the case.*

WHAT I'VE SEEN: The Client Who Assumed Wrong

Patricia walked into my office believing her divorce would take three months. Her husband, Keith, had agreed to everything over the kitchen table—she keeps the house, he keeps his pension, they split custody. No lawyers needed, Keith said. Just paperwork. Patricia nearly signed the agreement Keith drafted. On a friend's advice, she brought it to me first. The house was worth $290,000 with a $210,000 mortgage—$80,000 in equity. Keith's pension, after twenty-two years of state employment, was valued at $410,000. The 'even split' Keith proposed would have given Patricia $80,000 and cost her access to $205,000 in retirement funds she was legally entitled to share. Keith knew the math. Patricia did not. The divorce took eight months instead of three. But Patricia left with her full share of the marital estate—because she stopped assuming and started preparing.

CHAPTER 2

How the Divorce Process Works — A Map of the Road Ahead

Fear thrives on uncertainty. When you do not know what comes next—what a filing means, what discovery demands, whether mediation is mandatory or optional, how long a trial actually lasts—every step feels like walking blindfolded across a highway. The legal system seems deliberately opaque, and for many clients, that opacity becomes its own source of trauma.

This chapter strips the mystery away. What follows is a plain-language walkthrough of the divorce process from the first filing through final judgment. Not every state follows the identical sequence, and local rules vary in ways your attorney will explain, but the essential architecture is remarkably consistent. Once you see it clearly, the process stops being a monster in the dark and becomes a road with turns you can anticipate.

Filing the Petition

One spouse initiates the divorce by filing a petition—sometimes called a complaint—with the court. The petition names both parties, identifies any minor children, and makes preliminary claims about custody, support, and property. Filing first does not guarantee a tactical edge, but it does give the filing spouse the opportunity to choose the jurisdiction, frame the initial narrative, and control the opening timeline.

Being the respondent—the one who receives the petition—can feel like falling behind. It is not. Respondents have full rights to contest every claim, file counter-petitions asserting their own demands, and shape the case from the moment they engage.

WHAT I'VE SEEN: Two Responses to the Same Envelope

On the same Friday afternoon, two clients in my firm were served with divorce petitions. Carl, upon reading the papers, drove to the family home, confronted his wife in front of their children, and withdrew $40,000 from the joint savings account before the bank closed. He texted his wife: 'You want to play dirty? Watch what happens next.' By Monday morning, Carl's wife had obtained an emergency restraining order, a temporary freeze on all joint accounts, and temporary primary custody. His first forty-eight hours of panic produced six months of legal damage. Victoria, served the same day, called her sister, cried for an hour, then began organizing. She secured copies of financial documents, noted account balances, and said nothing beyond 'I received the papers and I'll have my attorney contact yours.' At her first meeting Monday, she arrived with a folder containing tax returns, bank statements, and a one-page summary of her concerns. Her attorney later called it the most productive initial consultation of the year. Same envelope. Same shock. Two trajectories determined not by the facts of the case but by what each client did in the first forty-eight hours.

Service of Process

After filing, the petition must be formally delivered to the other spouse—a step called service of process. A sheriff, private process server, or in some jurisdictions a certified mailing handles this. Until service is completed, the court lacks authority over the respondent. Some spouses evade service deliberately, hoping to stall. Courts have mechanisms for this, including service by publication, but avoidance rarely produces a lasting advantage.

The Answer and Counter-Petition

The respondent files a written response—typically within twenty to thirty days, though deadlines differ by state. The answer addresses each claim in the petition: admitted, denied, or insufficient information to respond. Many respondents also file a counter-petition, which is their opportunity to assert independent claims for custody, support, property division, and other relief. Failing to respond on time can result in a default judgment, which allows the court to grant the petitioner everything they requested. Do not let deadlines pass. If you have been served, contact an attorney immediately.

Temporary Orders: The Status Quo Battle

Between the filing and the final trial—a gap that can span months or even years—the court issues temporary orders to maintain stability. These orders typically address who lives in the marital home, who pays the mortgage and utilities, how parenting time is allocated, whether interim child support or spousal support is required, and whether either party is restrained from dissipating assets, harassing the other, or removing children from the jurisdiction.

Temporary orders carry outsize importance. The arrangements they establish tend to become the baseline against which a judge measures any future request for change. A temporary order that gives one parent primary custody and the other alternating weekends can be extraordinarily difficult to undo at trial, because courts hesitate to disrupt a routine that children have adapted to—even if that routine was imposed provisionally. Take temporary hearings as seriously as the final trial. Many experienced attorneys consider them more consequential.

> **Core Principle:** *Temporary orders often become permanent orders wearing different clothes. Treat every provisional arrangement as though it may last for years—because it might.*

Discovery: Where Cases Are Made or Broken

Discovery is the formal process through which each side compels the other to disclose information. It is the investigative engine of litigation, and in financially contested divorces, it is frequently where the outcome is determined.

The primary discovery tools include interrogatories—written questions that must be answered under oath; requests for production—demands for documents such as bank statements, tax returns, business records, emails, and text messages; requests for admissions—statements the opposing party must admit or deny under oath; depositions—live, sworn testimony taken outside the courtroom, transcribed by a court reporter; and subpoenas—orders compelling banks, employers, or other third parties to produce records.

Most clients underestimate discovery. They view it as bureaucratic paperwork. It is not. Discovery is the phase where hidden accounts surface, income discrepancies appear, lies become provable, and the factual foundation for trial is assembled or undermined. Clients who participate fully, respond honestly, and work closely with their attorney during discovery position themselves to negotiate from strength or present a compelling case at trial. Clients who treat it as an annoyance pay for that attitude later.

WHAT I'VE SEEN: The LLC That Almost Disappeared

During discovery, Helen's attorney subpoenaed her husband Jerome's business banking records. Jerome owned a small construction company and had reported annual income of $78,000 on their joint returns for three years. The bank records told a different story. Payments from clients were being deposited into a second company—an LLC registered to Jerome's brother but controlled entirely by Jerome. That LLC received $140,000 to $190,000 annually in payments that never appeared on Jerome's tax returns or financial disclosure. A forensic accountant traced the money through three accounts, documented the pattern across four years, and prepared a report for trial. Jerome's actual income was roughly three times what he had reported. The court imputed the hidden income, imposed sanctions for fraudulent disclosure, and awarded Helen a disproportionate share of the estate. The discovery process—which Jerome had dismissed as 'just paperwork'—uncovered the money. Without it, Helen would have received support based on a fabricated income figure for the remainder of her children's minority.

✦ ✦ ✦

Mediation

Many jurisdictions require mediation before trial. Even where it is not mandatory, courts encourage it. Mediation places both parties in a room—or in separate rooms, in "caucus" style—with a neutral third party whose job is to facilitate agreement, not to decide anything.

Mediation works best when both parties are willing to negotiate honestly and have realistic expectations. It works poorly—and can be harmful—when one party uses the process to manipulate, stall, or intimidate. Cases involving domestic violence, severe power imbalances, or deeply entrenched high-conflict dynamics often require modified mediation protocols or alternative dispute resolution approaches. Chapter 33 addresses mediation preparation in detail.

✦ ✦ ✦

Settlement Negotiations

The overwhelming majority of divorces—estimates range from 90 to 95 percent—resolve through settlement rather than trial. Settlement can happen at any stage: before filing, during discovery, in mediation, on the courthouse steps minutes before trial begins, or anywhere in between.

The art of settlement is knowing when to accept a deal that gives you 80 percent of what you want and when to reject an offer that sounds reasonable but contains buried traps. It requires clear priorities, accurate financial information, and the emotional discipline to evaluate proposals on their merits rather than through the lens of anger or revenge. Settlements are not surrenders. They are agreements you help design—as opposed to judgments imposed by a judge working with limited time and incomplete information.

✦ ✦ ✦

Trial

When settlement fails, the case proceeds to trial. Divorce trials bear little resemblance to what television portrays. There is no jury. A single judge hears evidence, evaluates witnesses, reviews exhibits, and renders a decision—sometimes from the bench the same day, sometimes in a written ruling weeks later.

Trial proceeds through a structured sequence: opening statements by each attorney, the petitioner's case-in-chief (direct examination of witnesses, introduction of exhibits), cross-examination by the opposing attorney, the respondent's case, potential rebuttal, and closing arguments. The entire process may take half a day for a focused hearing or multiple days for a complex case.

What surprises most clients about trial is how compressed it feels. You may have lived through years of conflict, but the judge may allocate each side only a few hours to present everything. This compression makes preparation essential. The witnesses you call, the exhibits you present, and the testimony you give must be curated, rehearsed, and organized to deliver maximum impact in minimum time.

> **Core Principle:** *Trials reward the prepared and punish the disorganized. A strong case poorly presented loses to a weaker case presented with clarity and discipline.*

The Final Judgment

The judge issues a judgment—also called a decree or order—that resolves all contested issues: property division, spousal support, child support, custody, and any ancillary matters. The judgment is a binding legal order. It governs your obligations, your rights, and your co-parenting framework going forward. Understanding exactly what it says—and what it requires of you—is not optional.

Post-Judgment: Appeals and Modifications

Appeals challenge the legal correctness of the judge's ruling and are appropriate only where a genuine legal error occurred. They are expensive, slow, and rarely successful. Modifications, by contrast, ask the court to revisit a specific provision because circumstances have materially changed since the original judgment—a job loss, a relocation, a change in the child's needs, or a significant shift in income. Chapter 37 addresses both in detail.

Timeline Reality

Clients routinely underestimate how long divorce takes. An uncontested case with minimal assets may resolve in weeks. A contested case with moderate complexity typically spans six to eighteen months. High-conflict cases with extensive discovery, multiple hearings, custody evaluations, and trial preparation can stretch beyond two years.

Delays are not always adversarial. Court calendars are crowded. Judges have hundreds of cases. Discovery takes time. Evaluators have waiting lists. Accept the timeline early and channel your energy into preparation rather than frustration. The clients who use the waiting periods productively—organizing evidence, stabilizing routines, strengthening their emotional health—enter each hearing with a measurable advantage over those who spend the same months anxious and idle.

Core Principle: *Understanding the road ahead does not eliminate the difficulty of traveling it. But it replaces panic with anticipation—and anticipation is the raw material of preparation.*

CHAPTER 3

How Judges Decide Divorce Cases

The most dangerous assumption a divorce client can make is that the judge will somehow absorb the full truth of their marriage—the years of sacrifice, the broken promises, the hidden lies—through sheer proximity to the case. Judges do not operate that way. They operate within a system built on limited time, formal evidence, and statutory frameworks that may or may not align with your personal sense of justice.

Grasping how judges actually process information, weigh evidence, and reach decisions is the difference between a client who walks into court expecting vindication and a client who walks in armed with a strategy calibrated to the reality of how rulings are made.

The Judge's Perspective

Family court judges carry staggering caseloads. A judge handling your temporary hearing may have reviewed seven other cases that morning. By the time your matter is called, the judge has perhaps fifteen to thirty minutes for each side to present evidence, make arguments, and answer questions.

That compression shapes everything. A judge cannot absorb your twenty-year marital history in thirty minutes. What a judge can absorb is a focused, well-organized presentation of the most relevant facts, supported by credible documentation and delivered by a witness who appears calm, truthful, and self-aware.

The practical consequence: your case must be distilled. Every piece of evidence, every witness, and every statement of testimony should be selected for impact and relevance. The client who brings a binder of three hundred pages of text messages—unorganized, un-highlighted, with no index—communicates chaos. The client who brings the same evidence reduced to the twenty most compelling exchanges, tabbed and summarized, communicates competence. Judges notice this distinction instantly.

WHAT I'VE SEEN: The Box and the Binder

Two mothers appeared before the same judge in the same month, each alleging that the other parent's home was unsafe. The first arrived with a cardboard box containing over three hundred pages of text messages, printed in no particular order, with no index and no summary. When the judge asked her to identify the most relevant exchanges, she flipped through pages, growing flustered, unable to locate the messages she wanted. The judge gave her three minutes, then moved on. The second mother brought a tabbed binder. Section one: a two-page chronological summary of incidents. Section two: twenty-three relevant text exchanges, highlighted and annotated. Section three: school attendance records showing absences during the father's weeks. Section four: a pediatrician's letter documenting missed medications. The judge reviewed the binder in under ten minutes and asked detailed follow-up questions. Identical underlying concerns. One parent was taken seriously. The other was not. The difference was organization—nothing more.

Property Division: The Two Frameworks

Every state follows one of two basic approaches to dividing marital property.

Community property states (roughly nine, including California, Texas, Arizona, and Louisiana) presume that everything earned or acquired during the marriage belongs equally to both spouses, regardless of whose name is on the account or title. Division starts from a fifty-fifty baseline, with limited exceptions.

Equitable distribution states (the majority) divide marital property "equitably," which means fairly—but not necessarily equally. Judges consider a range of factors to determine what division is just under the circumstances.

Common factors in equitable distribution include the duration of the marriage, each spouse's income and earning capacity, contributions to the marriage (including homemaking and child-rearing), the age and health of each party, the economic circumstances of each spouse at the time of division, any history of dissipation or economic misconduct, and the tax consequences of proposed distributions.

The distinction between marital and separate property is critical under both frameworks. Property acquired before the marriage, gifts received by one spouse individually, and inheritances are typically classified as separate. However, when separate property is commingled with marital funds—deposited into a joint account, used to improve a marital home, or blended into a jointly managed investment portfolio—the separate character can be lost. Chapter 20 covers this in depth.

Spousal Support: What Courts Evaluate

Alimony decisions rest on two foundational questions: does one spouse have a legitimate need for financial assistance, and does the other spouse have the capacity to provide it?

Beyond that threshold, courts consider the length of the marriage (shorter marriages produce less support), the standard of living during the marriage, each spouse's income and earning potential, the requesting spouse's efforts toward self-sufficiency, the age and health of both parties, contributions to the other spouse's career or education, and in some states, marital fault.

The trend in modern family law moves toward rehabilitative support—temporary assistance intended to allow the lower-earning spouse to develop skills, training, or employment sufficient for self-support—rather than permanent, open-ended payments. Permanent alimony still exists but is typically reserved for long marriages where one spouse has limited earning capacity due to age, health, or a decades-long absence from the workforce.

Child Support: The Calculation

Child support formulas are more mechanical than most other divorce determinations. Most states apply guidelines that calculate an amount based on the parents' combined income, the number of children, and the custody arrangement. Deviations from the guideline amount are possible but require specific justification.

Disputes about child support almost always involve disputes about income. A self-employed spouse who controls their own books can adjust reported earnings. A spouse who voluntarily reduces income—quitting a job, declining promotions, choosing underemployment—may face imputed income: the court assigns an earning figure based on what that person could reasonably earn, rather than what they choose to earn.

Custody: The Best-Interest Standard

When children are involved, the court's overriding focus shifts to the best interests of the child—a standard that encompasses safety, stability, the quality of each parent's relationship with the child, the ability to meet daily needs, emotional maturity, willingness to support the child's relationship with the other parent, and the child's own preferences (at appropriate ages).

Part III of this volume covers custody fundamentals. The companion volume, "Winning High-Conflict Custody Battles," provides the comprehensive treatment.

Credibility: The Currency of the Courtroom

In every contested divorce case I have tried, there comes a moment when the judge must choose whom to believe. Documents conflict. Testimony diverges. Both sides present versions of events that cannot coexist. At that inflection point, the decision almost always turns on which witness the judge finds more believable.

Credibility is built through consistency—saying the same thing in your deposition, your financial disclosure, your testimony, and your communications. It is built through composure—remaining measured under cross-examination when opposing counsel is deliberately trying to provoke an emotional eruption. It is built through honesty—acknowledging imperfections and mistakes rather than constructing an implausible portrait of yourself as faultless.

And credibility is destroyed with startling speed. A single provable lie undermines everything else you say. An emotional outburst on the witness stand erases hours of careful preparation. A social media post contradicting your sworn financial disclosure can dismantle a case that was otherwise strong.

> **Core Principle:** *Judges remember who was calm, who was honest even when it hurt, and who demonstrated the maturity to acknowledge imperfection. Those qualities earn trust. Trust determines outcomes.*

What Judges Notice That Attorneys Rarely Mention

In addition to evidence and testimony, judges observe subtleties that most clients never consider:

- How you enter the courtroom—do you look composed or agitated?

- Whether you make eye contact when answering questions or look away evasively

- How you react physically when your spouse testifies—do you shake your head, roll your eyes, whisper angrily to your attorney?

- Whether your clothing and demeanor suggest respect for the proceedings

- How you treat court staff, opposing counsel, and even your own attorney

- Whether you can acknowledge any fault at all—or whether you present yourself as entirely blameless

- Whether your children appear to be genuinely at the center of your concerns or merely a rhetorical device

None of this appears in a statute. All of it influences a judge's perception of who you are and whether you can be trusted with significant decisions about your family's future.

The Myth of "Fairness"

Nearly every divorce client arrives believing that fairness will prevail. The problem is that fairness, as you define it, may bear little resemblance to fairness as the law defines it.

You may feel that your spouse's affair entitles you to a larger share of the assets. In most equitable distribution states, adultery has minimal impact on property division. You may feel that twenty years of homemaking should guarantee lifetime support. The law may provide only a few years of rehabilitative payments. You may feel that a spouse who lied under oath should be stripped of custody. The court may focus on the children's attachment and daily routine rather than the parent's dishonesty in legal proceedings.

Accepting the gap between your sense of justice and the legal framework's definition of equity is one of the most difficult emotional tasks in divorce. It is also one of the most important. Clients who orient their expectations around what the law actually provides—rather than what they feel they deserve—make better decisions, settle more favorably, and spend far less on litigation driven by righteous indignation.

> **Core Principle:** *Judges apply the law to the facts. The law may disappoint you. Knowing that in advance is not cynicism—it is preparation.*

CHAPTER 4

Toxic Personalities and High-Conflict Tactics in Divorce

Not every divorce involves a difficult personality. Many end with sadness, negotiation, and an imperfect but workable resolution. If your case falls into that category, you may skim this chapter and move on.

But if you are divorcing someone who lies with breathtaking ease, who twists your words until you doubt your own memory, who presents a polished public image while behaving destructively in private, who treats the legal process as a weapon rather than a resolution mechanism—then this chapter was written for you.

Recognizing the Pattern

High-conflict personalities in divorce share recognizable behavioral signatures. Not every person with these traits has a diagnosable disorder—and I am not in the business of diagnosing anyone. What I can tell you, after watching thousands of contested cases, is that certain patterns recur with striking consistency.

Blame without exception. Nothing is ever their fault. If the marriage failed, you caused it. If the children are struggling, your parenting is the reason. If they behaved badly, you provoked them.

Accountability is not merely avoided—it is psychologically inconceivable to them.

Charm that disarms. In public—at school events, at social gatherings, in the lobby outside the courtroom—they are warm, engaging, and convincing. Mediators, evaluators, and even judges can be initially taken in by the performance. The gap between the public persona and the private reality is one of the most disorienting experiences their partners describe.

Narrative control. They rewrite history fluently. Events you witnessed firsthand are reframed, minimized, or flatly denied. Over time, this produces a creeping self-doubt in their partner: "Did that actually happen the way I remember?" It did. But the distortion is deliberate, and it serves to maintain the power imbalance.

Escalation as strategy. When they feel a loss of control—you set a boundary, you retained an attorney, you stopped responding to provocations—they escalate. Emergency custody motions filed without genuine emergency. False allegations timed to coincide with your important hearing. Police called to create a record that does not reflect reality. Escalation is not reactive anger. It is a calculated response to the threat of losing dominance.

Exhaustion as a weapon. They generate conflict faster than you can address it. New accusations arrive before the last ones are resolved. Legal filings multiply. Communication threads become unmanageable. The goal is not to win any single issue—it is to drain your resources, your emotional reserves, and your will to continue fighting.

WHAT I'VE SEEN: The Charmer and the Shadow

In the courthouse hallway, Kevin was warm, self-deprecating, and cooperative. He greeted opposing counsel with a handshake, complimented the mediator's patience, and told the evaluator he 'just wanted what was best for the kids.' His wife, Lauren, appeared tense, exhausted, and raw—which Kevin's attorney used to portray her as the unstable party. Then the text messages were introduced. Over fourteen months, Kevin had sent Lauren more than two thousand messages. The tone bore no resemblance to the man in the hallway. 'You are nothing without me.' 'No judge will believe you.' 'I will make sure you regret this.' Messages at 2 AM, 3 AM, 4 AM—sometimes fifteen in a single night. When Lauren stopped responding, Kevin messaged through the children: 'Tell your mother she needs to answer me.' The evaluator revised the report. Kevin's public warmth and his 2 AM campaigns could not coexist without one being fabricated. The evaluator concluded that Kevin's public persona was constructed, his private conduct was controlling, and Lauren's visible exhaustion was the predictable result of sustained psychological aggression—not instability. Kevin's performance was flawless. His text messages told the truth.

DARVO: The Manipulation Pattern Courts See Constantly

DARVO stands for Deny, Attack, Reverse Victim and Offender. It is among the most common manipulation sequences in high-conflict divorce.

Deny: "I never said that." "That never happened." "You're making things up."

Attack: "You're the one who's unstable." "Everyone knows you're the problem." "I'm going to make sure the judge sees what you really are."

Reverse Victim and Offender: "I'm the one being abused here." "You drove me to this." "I had to file the protective order because I was afraid of you."

When DARVO is operating, the person who caused harm presents as the victim, and the actual victim is cast as the aggressor. In courtrooms where judges have limited time to evaluate complex interpersonal dynamics, this reversal can be devastatingly effective—at least initially. The antidote is documentation. A pattern of DARVO behavior, captured in contemporaneous records over time, becomes visible to judges and evaluators who know what to look for.

The Narcissistic Pattern in Divorce

Among the personality patterns that surface in contested cases, narcissistic traits appear with conspicuous frequency. A spouse operating from narcissistic patterns typically displays extreme self-focus—everything revolves around their image, their feelings, their version of events. The child's actual needs become secondary to the narrative the narcissistic parent is constructing.

They manage impressions relentlessly. To the custody evaluator, they are the devoted parent. On social media, they are the beleaguered hero. In text messages to you—unseen by the audience—they are controlling, threatening, and contemptuous.

They view the divorce as a zero-sum competition. Shared custody feels like losing. Your success in any aspect of the case feels like a personal attack. Compromise registers as humiliation. This makes settlement extraordinarily difficult, because the narcissistic spouse cannot tolerate any outcome that does not feel like total victory.

If this description resonates, the most important thing I can tell you is this: you cannot reason your way out of it. You cannot explain clearly enough to make them see your perspective. You cannot be accommodating enough to earn cooperation. The strategies that work with reasonable people—empathy, compromise, appeals to the children's welfare—are interpreted as weakness by a narcissistic personality and exploited accordingly.

The Gray Rock Method

Gray rock is a communication approach built on the principle of becoming as unremarkable and uninteresting to the high-conflict person as a gray rock on the ground. You provide no emotional reaction. No defensiveness. No detailed explanations. No fuel for the fire.

In practice, this means responding to provocative messages with brief, factual, emotionally flat replies—or not responding at all when no response is required. It means declining to engage with accusations, insults, or bait. It means keeping every interaction transactional rather than emotional.

Gray rock is not passivity. It is a deliberate, disciplined refusal to participate in the conflict cycle that high-conflict personalities depend on. When you stop providing the reaction they crave, two things happen: they often escalate initially (because the old tactics are not working), and then, over time, they redirect their energy elsewhere—or their escalation is documented and becomes evidence of their own instability.

> **Core Principle:** *You cannot reform a high-conflict personality through the divorce process. You can only control what you say, what you write, and how you present yourself—and build a factual record that speaks louder than their performance.*

For comprehensive coverage of toxic personality tactics in custody disputes specifically, see Chapters 2 and 12 of the companion volume, "Winning High-Conflict Custody Battles."

CHAPTER 5

Myths That Destroy Divorce Cases

I have watched more cases damaged by what clients believed than by what their opponents did. False assumptions about how courts operate, what judges value, and what the law actually says produce strategic errors that no attorney can fully repair. The myths in this chapter are not obscure technicalities. They are beliefs I encounter weekly—held by intelligent, well-meaning people who absorbed them from friends, family, the internet, or outdated cultural assumptions.

Each one has cost real clients real money, real custody time, or real credibility. Read them with the willingness to abandon whatever you thought you knew and replace it with what actually happens inside courtrooms.

Myth 1: "The Judge Will See Through My Spouse's Lies"

This is the single most dangerous belief in family law. Clients cling to it because it offers comfort: surely the truth will prevail on its own.

It does not. Judges are experienced, but they are not omniscient. They see carefully curated presentations from both sides, not the raw, unedited reality of your marriage. A spouse who lies convincingly—and many do—can create reasonable doubt about your version of events unless you bring organized, credible evidence to counter the fabrication.

The truth does not announce itself. It must be demonstrated through documentation, corroborating witnesses, financial records, and calm, consistent testimony. Hope is not a litigation strategy.

WHAT I'VE SEEN: The Case That Had No Evidence

Yvonne knew her ex-husband, Derek, was drinking again. She smelled it at exchanges. The children mentioned Daddy 'fell asleep on the couch before dinner' three times in one month. At the temporary hearing, Yvonne's attorney sought court-ordered substance testing. Derek's attorney asked: 'Where is the evidence?' Yvonne had no log. No photographs. No corroborating texts. No medical or school records. She had her own observations and her children's offhand comments—neither sufficient for court-ordered testing. The motion was denied. Six months later, Yvonne returned transformed. She had maintained a contemporaneous log documenting fourteen specific instances. She had preserved texts where Derek admitted to 'having a few' during his parenting time. She had a letter from the school counselor noting the children's increased anxiety on Monday mornings following Derek's weekends. The motion was granted. Soberlink monitoring was ordered. Two positive results followed within six weeks, and overnights were suspended pending treatment. The truth was identical in both hearings. The evidence was not.

Myth 2: "Infidelity Means I Win Everything"

Discovering your spouse's affair feels like it should change the legal calculus entirely. In most states, it barely moves the needle. The majority of jurisdictions follow no-fault divorce laws, which means the court divides property and determines support based on statutory factors—not on who broke the marriage vows.

Infidelity can matter in limited ways: if marital funds were spent on the affair partner (dissipation), if the affair exposed children to inappropriate situations, or if the affair is relevant to a fault-based alimony claim in states that still recognize marital fault. But the idea that an unfaithful spouse will be "punished" through a radically unfavorable property division or custody outcome is, in most jurisdictions, a fantasy that leads to expensive litigation and bitter disappointment.

Myth 3: "I'll Get Half of Everything"

In community property states, a fifty-fifty starting point exists for marital assets—but even there, specific circumstances can alter the split. In equitable distribution states, "equitable" means fair, not equal. A judge may award 60-40, 70-30, or another ratio based on the specific factors governing that jurisdiction.

And "everything" is itself a loaded word. Only marital property is subject to division. Separate property—assets owned before the marriage, individual gifts, inheritances kept apart from joint funds—generally remains with the spouse who holds it. The classification fight between marital and separate property consumes enormous attorney hours in complex cases and can radically alter the outcome.

♦ ♦ ♦

Myth 4: "If I Leave the House, I Lose It"

Clients stay in miserable or even dangerous living situations because someone told them that moving out forfeits their claim to the marital home. This is almost never true as a matter of property law. The home's classification as marital property and its value in the overall distribution are not determined by who sleeps there.

Where departure can matter is custody. A parent who moves out of the family home and into an apartment while the children remain with the other parent has, in practical terms, conceded the status quo. Courts observe the existing arrangement and may be reluctant to disrupt it. If you are contemplating a move, consult your attorney about the custody implications before you sign a lease.

Myth 5: "The Kids Can Choose Who They Live With"

Children do not choose their custodial parent. In some states, once a child reaches a certain age—often twelve, thirteen, or fourteen—the court may consider the child's stated preference as one factor among many. The preference is never dispositive, and judges evaluate whether the stated preference reflects genuine attachment and well-being or coaching, fear, bribery, or alignment with the more permissive parent.

Telling your child that they "get to choose" burdens them with a decision no child should carry and may expose you to allegations of coaching or alienation. Let the court handle this.

Myth 6: "My Spouse Will Pay All My Attorney's Fees"

Courts can order one party to contribute to the other's legal fees, but this is discretionary and typically reserved for situations involving a significant income disparity, bad-faith litigation conduct, or a demonstrated inability to afford representation. The default expectation is that each side covers their own costs. Budget accordingly and do not litigate on the assumption that your spouse will eventually foot the bill.

Myth 7: "I Don't Need a Lawyer for a Simple Divorce"

Some divorces are genuinely simple enough to resolve with minimal legal involvement—particularly those with no children, no significant assets, and no contested issues. But the definition of "simple" is narrower than most people realize.

The moment your case involves retirement account division, real property, business interests, spousal support, contested custody, or any financial complexity, the risks of self-representation multiply sharply. A poorly drafted settlement agreement can cost you tens of thousands of dollars over its lifetime. A missed QDRO (the order required to divide retirement accounts) can leave a substantial asset completely unaddressed. The money saved by forgoing an attorney is frequently dwarfed by the money lost through errors the attorney would have prevented.

Myth 8: "Mediation Means I Have to Give In"

Mediation is not arbitration. The mediator has no power to impose a result. If you walk into mediation prepared—with clear priorities, documented financial information, and a firm understanding of your bottom line—you retain full control over whether to accept or reject any proposal. Mediation simply provides a structured environment for negotiation. Effective mediation can produce outcomes both parties can live with at a fraction of the cost and emotional damage of trial.

Myth 9: "Once We Settle, It's Over Forever"

Property division provisions in a settlement are generally final and cannot be reopened absent fraud or extraordinary circumstances.

But custody, child support, and in many cases spousal support are modifiable when a material change in circumstances occurs. A settlement is a resolution—not a permanent seal. Understanding what can be revisited later and what cannot should inform every decision you make during negotiations.

Myth 10: "Social Media Is My Private Space"

Nothing you post online during a divorce is private. Not your Instagram stories. Not your locked-down Facebook profile. Not your Snapchat messages that supposedly disappear. Not your private DMs. Courts admit social media evidence routinely. Opposing counsel can subpoena your accounts. Mutual friends screenshot and forward. Privacy settings create an illusion of protection that evaporates the moment someone takes a screenshot.

A photograph of you at a bar contradicts your claim of sobriety. A vacation post undercuts your assertion that you cannot afford support. An angry rant about your spouse becomes Exhibit A in their motion to restrict your custody. Chapter 9 provides a complete social media protocol for litigation. For now, the rule is simple: if you would not say it standing in front of the judge, do not put it anywhere a screen can capture it.

Myth 11: "The Court System Will
Be Quick About This"

It will not. Family courts are overcrowded, understaffed, and processing more cases than the system was designed to handle. Hearings get continued. Trial dates get pushed. Evaluator reports take months. The spouse who enters the process expecting swift resolution and encounters delay after delay becomes frustrated, then despondent, then reckless. The client who accepts the timeline early and uses the interim productively—gathering evidence, building emotional resilience, organizing financial records—turns the court's pace into an advantage.

> **Core Principle:** *What you believe about divorce matters as much as what you know. Replace every myth with the reality it conceals, and you eliminate half the mistakes most clients make before they ever enter a courtroom.*

WHAT I'VE SEEN: The Client Who Believed All of Them

Thomas arrived at his first consultation armed with five unshakable beliefs: his wife's affair entitled him to the house, the children would choose to live with him, the judge would see through his wife's manipulations without evidence, the case would resolve in three months, and his social media commentary was protected speech. Within six months, every belief had met reality. The affair had no bearing on property division in his state. His twelve-year-old's preference was one factor among twelve, and the child appeared coached. His wife presented organized documentation while Thomas presented emotion. The case took fourteen months. And a Facebook post calling his wife 'a sociopath who doesn't deserve custody' was read aloud at the temporary hearing, prompting the judge to observe that Thomas 'demonstrates poor judgment regarding the impact of public statements on the children.' Thomas was not a bad father. He was an unprepared one. Every myth he carried produced a specific, measurable mistake. By the time he abandoned those beliefs, he had lost six months of positioning he never fully recovered.

Emotional regulation and communication discipline are your first line of defense. Master these before engaging on any contested issue.

PART II

YOUR MINDSET, CREDIBILITY, AND EMOTIONAL STRATEGY

The four chapters ahead address something most divorce books ignore entirely: the psychological architecture that separates clients who protect their position from those who sabotage it. Your emotional state is not a sidebar to your legal case. It is a variable that judges, evaluators, and opposing counsel observe and exploit. Mastering it gives you an edge that no amount of money or legal firepower can replicate.

CHAPTER 6

Staying Stable When Everything Is Unstable

At three in the morning, your phone buzzes. Another message from your spouse—accusatory, venomous, crafted to detonate something inside you. Your heart pounds. Your hands shake. Every fiber of your body screams at you to respond, to defend yourself, to fire back with equal fury.

That impulse, if followed, may become the single most damaging piece of evidence in your case.

The collision between emotional reality and legal necessity is the defining tension of divorce. You are enduring one of the most destabilizing experiences a human being can face, and the system demands that you present yourself as composed, reasonable, and measured—often in the same week you discover your spouse emptied a bank account, filed a false police report, or told your child you do not love them.

Unfair? Absolutely. Irrelevant? Not even slightly. Because how you manage yourself under that pressure communicates more to a judge than any argument your attorney will ever make.

Your Emotional State Is Under a Microscope

Judges do not have the luxury of observing your marriage over twenty years. They get snapshots—a hearing, a report from an evaluator, a stack of text messages, a few hours of testimony. In those compressed windows, your demeanor communicates volumes. A parent who appears calm, organized, and self-aware earns trust. A parent who appears volatile, defensive, or consumed by bitterness triggers concern.

Custody evaluators, guardians ad litem, therapists, mediators, and even opposing counsel are assessing your emotional regulation in every interaction. The evaluator who visits your home notices whether you speak about your spouse with restrained concern or seething contempt. The mediator notices whether you can acknowledge any validity in your spouse's position or whether you categorically dismiss everything they say. Your own attorney notices whether you can follow advice or whether you override it with emotional impulses.

None of this is about performing. Authentic composure—the kind rooted in genuine self-awareness rather than suppressed rage—is visible and convincing. Manufactured calm, layered over unprocessed fury, cracks under the smallest pressure. The distinction is real, and professionals detect it.

What Stress Does to Your Brain

Sustained conflict triggers a neurological cascade that works against your interests. When your nervous system perceives threat—a hostile text, a court date, an accusation—your body floods with cortisol and adrenaline. Decision-making shifts from the prefrontal cortex (where logic, planning, and impulse control reside) to the amygdala (where fight-or-flight reactions originate).

In that state, you are physiologically wired to react rather than reflect. Your memory narrows. Your ability to evaluate risk deteriorates. You become more likely to send the retaliatory message, make the impulsive financial decision, or say the regrettable thing in front of witnesses.

This is not a character flaw. It is biology. And recognizing it is the first step toward managing it. When you feel the surge—the pounding heart, the tunnel vision, the overwhelming urge to act immediately—that is your cue to stop, not to go.

The Three Pillars of Emotional Resilience in Divorce

Across thousands of cases, the clients who maintained their composure through sustained conflict shared three characteristics. None of them were naturally unflappable. All of them built these capacities deliberately.

Pillar 1: Detachment from the Chaos

Detachment does not mean indifference. It means refusing to let your spouse's behavior govern your emotional state. When your spouse sends a provocative message, detachment asks: "Does this require a response? If so, what response serves my interests?" rather than "How dare they say that to me?"

Detachment is the internal decision to stop trying to change, educate, or reason with someone who has demonstrated they cannot be changed, educated, or reasoned with. It is the recognition that engaging emotionally with a person who feeds on conflict is a losing proposition every single time.

Pillar 2: Disciplined Self-Regulation

The 30-Minute Rule. When a hostile message arrives, do not touch your phone for thirty minutes. Walk away. Breathe. Let the adrenaline subside. Return only when your prefrontal cortex has re-engaged. This single habit prevents more self-inflicted damage than any other tool I have encountered.

The Courtroom Camera Test. Before sending any message, posting anything online, or making any decision during your case, imagine a camera recording the moment for a judge's review. If the footage would make you look unhinged, petty, vindictive, or reckless—stop.

Two-Column Thinking. Divide a page. Left column: what you feel like doing. Right column: what actually serves your case. Write both. Choose the right column. Every time. The left column is your pressure valve. The right column is your strategy.

Pillar 3: Anchoring to What Matters

In the heat of conflict, perspective collapses. A disputed weekend exchange feels like the defining battle of the case. An insulting text feels like it demands an immediate, devastating response. A minor procedural setback feels like total defeat.

Anchoring is the practice of repeatedly returning to the questions that actually matter: What outcome am I working toward? What does my child need from me today? Will this issue matter in five years? If the answer is no, conserve your energy for the fights that will.

Therapy Is Not a Concession—It Is an Investment

I have watched clients resist therapy with the same ferocity they bring to the courtroom. They worry it will be perceived as weakness. They fear a therapist's notes could be subpoenaed and used against them. They believe they should be able to handle this on their own.

Here is what I have seen across four decades: the clients who engage in therapy consistently outperform those who refuse it. Not because therapy is magic, but because it provides a contained, private space to process the emotional weight that otherwise leaks into texts, courtroom behavior, and decision-making. It gives you a place to fall apart so you do not fall apart in front of people who are evaluating you.

Judges view therapy favorably. A parent who seeks support demonstrates insight, humility, and responsibility. A parent who insists they need no help while visibly struggling raises red flags about self-awareness.

Discuss with your attorney what to share and what to approach cautiously in sessions. Therapy records can be discoverable in some jurisdictions. This is manageable—but it requires awareness.

Building Your Support Circle

Not everyone in your life helps during divorce. Some friends amplify your anger. Some family members give catastrophic legal advice gleaned from their own cases in a different state twenty years ago. Some people mean well but lack the capacity to offer anything beyond confirmation of your worst fears.

You need people who ground you, not people who ignite you. A small circle of steady, trustworthy individuals—a therapist, one or two friends who listen without escalating, perhaps a support group of people in similar situations—is worth more than a hundred sympathetic acquaintances who validate your rage.

WHAT I'VE SEEN: The Sister Who Kept the Fire Burning

Megan's sister, Jill, monitored the ex-husband's social media obsessively and forwarded every post to Megan—sometimes five or six times a day. A restaurant photo with an unrecognized woman. A weekend trip with the children Megan hadn't heard about. A comment on a mutual friend's page that could be read as a dig. Each forwarded message sent Megan spiraling. Her sleep deteriorated. Her work suffered. She began drafting retaliatory texts she barely stopped herself from sending. At exchanges, her agitation was visible to the children, who started asking if Mommy was okay. Megan's attorney recommended one change: tell Jill to stop. Completely. After a particularly bad week in which forwarded posts triggered a panic attack before a mediation session, Megan set the boundary. Within two weeks, her sleep improved. Within a month, her attorney noticed measurable composure in her communications. The evaluator noted that Megan 'appeared significantly more regulated and child-focused than in previous interactions.' Nothing had changed except the information Megan was voluntarily consuming. The fire was real. Jill had been supplying the oxygen.

The Self-Medication Trap

Alcohol consumption increases during divorce. So does reliance on prescription medications, sleep aids, and other substances that dull the pain. The temptation is understandable. The consequences are severe.

A DUI during custody litigation can reshape the entire case. A pattern of increased drinking documented through receipts, bar check-ins, or witness testimony hands opposing counsel a narrative that is difficult to dismantle. Prescription misuse, even when the medication was legitimately prescribed, can become an issue if it affects your judgment or parenting capacity.

If you are struggling with substance use—or if the stress of the case has pushed existing consumption patterns into dangerous territory—address it now, before it addresses you in a courtroom. Treatment is viewed favorably. Denial is viewed with alarm.

> **Core Principle:** *Your emotional state is not separate from your case. It is the lens through which every judge, evaluator, and professional perceives everything else about you. Guard it with the same intensity you bring to guarding your financial records.*

CHAPTER 7

Thinking Like a Strategic Client

Most people who enter divorce think like wounded spouses. They think about what is fair, what they deserve, what their partner did wrong, and what punishment the system should impose. They bring their emotional injury into every meeting with their attorney, every communication with their spouse, and every appearance before the court.

The clients who achieve the strongest outcomes think differently. They think like litigants.

The Shift from Emotional Participant to Prepared Litigant

A litigant does not ask "Is this fair?" A litigant asks "Can I prove it? What does the evidence show? How will a judge evaluate this? What will it cost to fight over this issue, and is the potential gain worth the expenditure?"

This shift is not cold or heartless. It is the most protective thing you can do for yourself and your children. Emotional decision-making in divorce produces scorched-earth litigation strategies that bankrupt both parties, custody fights over relatively minor scheduling details that cost ten thousand dollars per disputed hour, retaliatory motions that impress no one and drain everyone, and settlements rejected not because they were bad but because accepting them felt like losing.

Thinking like a litigant means evaluating every decision through a cost-benefit lens. The question is never "What do I want?" alone. The question is "What do I want, what will it cost to get it, what is the probability of success, and what am I sacrificing by pursuing it?"

Choosing Your Battles

One of the most valuable things an experienced attorney tells a client is: "You can fight over this. But should you?"

Every contested issue consumes three resources: money, time, and emotional capital. A dispute over who keeps the living room furniture may cost more in attorney fees than the furniture is worth. A fight over whether your child attends soccer practice on your weekend or your spouse's may require a motion, a hearing, and two thousand dollars in legal fees to resolve something a simple conversation could have handled.

The clients who emerge from divorce in the strongest position are ruthless about prioritization. They identify the three or four issues that genuinely matter—primary custody, the marital home, a fair share of retirement assets, protection from an abusive or addicted spouse—and they invest their resources there. Everything else is negotiable.

This does not mean capitulating on every secondary issue. It means approaching them with flexibility and pragmatism rather than the emotional rigidity that turns every minor disagreement into a major conflict.

The Credibility Account

Think of your credibility with the court as a bank account. Every action you take either adds to the balance or subtracts from it. A calm, factual response to a hostile message is a deposit. An emotional tirade in reply is a withdrawal. Complying with a court order you disagree with is a deposit. Violating it because your spouse violated theirs is a withdrawal. Acknowledging an imperfection honestly is a deposit. Presenting yourself as flawless is a withdrawal.

The balance in that account at the time of trial determines how much trust the judge extends to your testimony, your claims, and your requests. Clients who accumulate deposits over months arrive at trial with a reservoir of goodwill. Clients who make repeated withdrawals arrive with a deficit that no closing argument can repair.

Being the Client Your Attorney Needs

Attorneys rarely say this aloud, but every family law practitioner knows the difference between a client who strengthens the case and a client who makes it harder to win.

The strengthening client arrives at meetings with organized documents, communicates concerns in concise written summaries rather than meandering phone calls, follows advice even when it conflicts with their instincts, responds to discovery requests promptly, avoids creating new problems between hearings, and trusts the attorney to handle legal strategy while they focus on the daily conduct that shapes the judge's perception.

The undermining client calls multiple times a day with non-emergencies, ignores counsel and fires off emotional messages to their spouse, posts inflammatory content on social media despite repeated warnings, refuses to organize financial documents, makes unilateral decisions about custody exchanges, and second-guesses every legal recommendation based on advice from a friend whose case in another state bore no resemblance to theirs.

Be the first client. Your attorney is working for you, but they work best when you are rowing in the same direction.

WHAT I'VE SEEN: The Organized Client and the Chaotic One

Ellen and Donna had virtually identical cases: ten-year marriages, two children, mid-range incomes, moderately contested custody. Their attorneys billed at the same hourly rate. Ellen maintained a binder with tabbed sections, sent concise emails, and responded to discovery within days. She followed advice even when it conflicted with her instincts. Her case resolved in eleven months. Total fees: $18,500. Donna called her attorney three to five times weekly about non-emergencies. She forwarded every hostile message with 'CAN YOU BELIEVE THIS?' generating billable time that produced no value. She ignored social media warnings and posted about her husband's affair—which became an exhibit. She refused to organize financial records, forcing her attorney to subpoena documents sitting in Donna's own filing cabinet. She rejected two reasonable settlements because accepting felt like losing. Her case went to trial after nineteen months. Total fees: $67,000. Same case. Same firm. Same rate. A $48,500 difference driven entirely by client behavior.

Core Principle: *The most formidable divorce clients are not the wealthiest or the angriest. They are the ones who treat their case like the consequential legal proceeding it is—with discipline, organization, and the willingness to subordinate emotion to strategy.*

CHAPTER 8

Communication Discipline — Every Word Is a Potential Exhibit

In my first decade of practice, the most damaging evidence in divorce cases came from financial records and witness testimony. Today, the evidence that destroys the most cases comes from the clients themselves—from their text messages, their emails, their voicemails, and their social media posts.

We live in an era of permanent written records. Every message you send your spouse during this case is preserved, searchable, and admissible. Opposing counsel will mine your text threads the way a forensic accountant mines bank statements—looking for the message that contradicts your sworn testimony, reveals your temper, demonstrates poor judgment, or proves you violated a court order.

The discipline of communication during divorce is not about being fake. It is about being intentional. Every word you choose either advances your position or undermines it. There is no neutral ground.

The BIFF Method

The most reliable framework for communicating with a difficult spouse during litigation is BIFF, developed by Bill Eddy of the

High Conflict Institute. The acronym stands for Brief, Informative, Friendly, and Firm.

Brief. Two to five sentences. No more. Long messages signal emotional flooding. They give the other side ammunition, quotes to extract out of context, and evidence that you cannot regulate yourself. Say what needs to be said and stop.

Informative. Facts and logistics only. No feelings. No accusations. No history lessons. No sarcasm. The purpose of the message is to convey necessary information about the children, the schedule, or a logistical matter—not to win an argument.

Friendly. Or at minimum, neutral. A tone of basic civility is not a gift to your spouse. It is an investment in your own credibility. Judges read text threads and form instant impressions. The parent who maintains a professional tone, even under provocation, looks like the adult in the room.

Firm. Clear boundaries stated without aggression. "I am not available to switch the schedule this weekend" is firm. "Absolutely not, you always pull this garbage" is reactive. Both decline the request. Only one protects your case.

BIFF in Action

Their message: "You're a terrible parent. The kids hate being at your house. I'm going to make sure the judge hears about all the neglect."

Reactive response (damages your case): "Are you kidding me? YOU're the one who can't be bothered to show up to a single school event. The kids love being here. You're delusional and I'm going to prove it."

BIFF response (strengthens your case): "The children are safe and well. I'm happy to discuss any specific concerns through our attorneys or a family therapist."

Read both again. One sounds like a parent in control. The other sounds like a participant in the chaos. A judge reading the thread draws conclusions before either attorney says a word.

When Silence Is the Strongest Response

Not every message requires a reply. A provocative text that contains no logistical question, no scheduling matter, and no information you need to address can simply be left unanswered. Silence is not evasion. It is the refusal to participate in a conflict cycle that serves only the person who initiated it.

Before responding to any message from your spouse, ask three questions: Does this require a response? If so, does it require a response right now? If so, what is the shortest, most factual response that addresses the actual issue?

If the answer to the first question is no, put the phone down and walk away. You have just won a small but meaningful battle—the battle against your own reactivity.

Co-Parenting Communication Platforms

OurFamilyWizard, TalkingParents, and AppClose create unalterable, timestamped records of every exchange. Messages cannot be deleted or edited after sending. Courts increasingly order their use in contested cases, and for good reason: they eliminate the "I never said that" defense entirely.

If your case involves any level of conflict, request that all parenting communication move to one of these platforms. The documentation they produce is worth its weight in depositions.

What to Say to Everyone Else

Your communication discipline extends beyond your spouse. What you tell friends, family members, coworkers, and acquaintances about your divorce can surface as evidence. A coworker who overhears you say, "I'm going to take him for everything he's worth," may be subpoenaed. A family member you confided in may be called to testify about your state of mind. A mutual friend may relay your comments directly to your spouse's attorney.

The operating principle is straightforward: say nothing about your divorce to anyone that you would not want repeated under oath. Your attorney and your therapist are the only two people to whom you should speak with full candor. Everyone else receives the neutral, restrained version.

> **Core Principle:** *Every message, email, voicemail, and offhand comment you make during this process is a potential courtroom exhibit. Communicate as if the judge is reading over your shoulder—because by the time this reaches trial, they may well be.*

A full library of communication scripts for specific divorce scenarios appears in Chapter 46. Additional custody-specific scripts appear in the companion volume, Part VII.

CHAPTER 9

Social Media and Your Digital Footprint

In 2008, social media evidence was a novelty in family court. By 2015, it was common. Today, it is expected. Attorneys routinely demand production of social media content during discovery. Judges accept screenshots, posts, and even metadata as exhibits. And the volume of cases damaged or destroyed by a client's own online activity has reached a level that would have been unimaginable a decade ago.

If you retain nothing else from this chapter, retain this: everything you post, comment, like, share, message, or react to during your divorce exists in a permanent, discoverable, screenshotable form. Privacy settings do not protect you. Deletion after the fact may constitute spoliation of evidence. The illusion that social media is a private diary belongs to a world that no longer exists.

What Courts Admit

The list is broader than most clients realize:

- Public and private posts on any platform—Facebook, Instagram, TikTok, X, LinkedIn, Snapchat, Reddit, BeReal, Threads

- Stories and temporary content (screenshots captured by anyone who viewed them)

- Direct messages and group chats

- Dating app profiles and conversations (Tinder, Bumble, Hinge, and others)

- Check-ins and location tags

- Venmo, Cash App, and Zelle transaction histories (and the public-facing descriptions)

- Comments on other people's posts

- Photos and videos you are tagged in—even those you did not post

- Deleted content recovered through forensic examination

If it passed through a screen, it can reach a courtroom.

The Posts That Destroy Cases

Certain categories of social media content inflict disproportionate damage, and I have watched each of them derail otherwise strong cases:

Photos involving alcohol during parenting time. A glass of wine at dinner may be innocent. A photograph of that glass, posted to Instagram on a night your custody schedule shows the children are with you, becomes an exhibit in a substance abuse argument. Context evaporates in a courtroom.

Disparagement of your spouse—direct or indirect. Naming them is bad. Vague posts clearly aimed at them are barely better. "Some people will never change" posted after a contentious exchange is transparent to everyone, including the judge. Memes mocking your ex, hashtags like #narcissist or #toxicex, and "cryptic" quotes that your entire social circle can decode all damage your credibility.

Lifestyle posts that contradict your financial claims. If you told the court you cannot afford spousal support, a vacation photo from Cancun becomes Exhibit B. If you claimed modest income, a post showing a new vehicle raises questions your attorney cannot easily answer.

Celebration of legal victories. "Justice was served today" after a favorable hearing makes you look like someone who views this as a game to be won rather than a family to be sorted. Judges notice.

Posts involving your children. A child's distress at exchanges, their reluctance to visit the other parent, their private struggles—none of this belongs on social media. Posting it suggests that your need for validation outweighs your child's privacy.

New relationship announcements. Introducing a new partner on social media before the divorce is final—or worse, before temporary orders are resolved—hands opposing counsel a narrative about your priorities, your judgment, and your timeline. Even if the relationship is genuine and healthy, the optics during active litigation are uniformly bad.

✦ ✦ ✦

The Deletion Trap

A reflexive instinct when clients realize their social media is vulnerable is to delete everything. This is often a mistake—and can be a serious one. Once litigation has commenced, you may be subject to a duty to preserve relevant evidence. Deleting posts, messages, or accounts after filing—or after learning that a case is imminent—can constitute spoliation: the intentional destruction of evidence.

Courts respond to spoliation with adverse inferences (allowing the judge to assume the deleted content was harmful), monetary sanctions, or other penalties. The content you deleted to protect yourself becomes a weapon used against you—not because of what it said, but because you tried to hide it.

Consult your attorney before deleting anything. The safer path is to stop posting new content rather than to destroy what already exists.

◆ ◆ ◆

Your Social Media Protocol During Litigation

The strongest approach is the simplest: stop posting entirely until the case concludes. Deactivate your accounts or set them to maximum privacy and walk away. Silence is not suspicious. It is disciplined. Judges view a deliberate reduction in social media activity as evidence that a client takes the proceedings seriously.

If you choose to remain active online—for professional reasons or because complete withdrawal feels impossible—limit yourself to genuinely neutral content: professional accomplishments, inoffensive hobbies, community involvement, and nothing whatsoever related to your spouse, your children's private lives, your case, your legal strategy, or your personal life during the pendency of litigation.

No late-night posts. Emotional posts written after midnight are the social media equivalent of drunk dialing. They feel cathartic in the moment and catastrophic in the morning.

◆ ◆ ◆

Digital Forensics: What an Expert Can Find

If you believe your spouse has destroyed relevant digital evidence—deleted messages, erased financial apps, wiped a phone—a digital forensic examiner can often recover it. Deleted files leave traces. Cloud backups preserve what local deletion removes. Metadata embedded in photographs reveals when and where they were taken. Browser histories reconstruct patterns of activity even after the cache has been cleared.

Conversely, if you have destroyed digital evidence, understand that recovery is possible and your spouse's attorney may pursue it.

> **Core Principle:** *If you would not stand in open court and say it to the judge's face, do not put it anywhere a screen can capture it. Digital evidence is permanent evidence. Act accordingly.*

Custody outcomes reward the parent who demonstrates stability through evidence and maintains credibility under evaluation

PART III

CUSTODY: THE ESSENTIAL FOUNDATION

If you have children, nothing in this divorce matters more than what happens to them. Not the house. Not the retirement accounts. Not the principle of the thing. The arrangement you build for your children—where they sleep, who makes their medical decisions, how holidays are divided, and whether they grow up sheltered from the conflict or consumed by it—will define their childhood and echo into their adult lives.

The four chapters ahead give you a thorough grounding in custody law, child protection during divorce, the professionals who will evaluate your family, and the architecture of parenting plans that survive conflict. This section stands on its own. For readers facing high-conflict custody involving personality-disordered or deeply manipulative co-parents, I have written a separate, dedicated companion volume that goes deeper into alienation tactics and defenses, custody-specific courtroom testimony, advanced parallel parenting, and a full library of custody scripts and templates.

COMPANION VOLUME — For the deep dive, see Winning High-Conflict Custody Battles: A Trial Lawyer's Proven Front-Line Strategies to Protect Your Children and Your Case.

CHAPTER 10

Custody Fundamentals Every Divorcing Parent Must Understand

Before you can protect your position, you need to speak the language. Custody law carries its own vocabulary, its own presumptions, and its own logic—much of which runs counter to what parents absorb from cultural convention, television, or the advice of a well-meaning friend who went through a divorce in another state fifteen years ago.

Legal Custody vs. Physical Custody

Legal custody determines who makes the major decisions governing your child's life: education, medical treatment, religious upbringing, and extracurricular involvement. When legal custody is joint—the most common arrangement—both parents share that authority. In practice, neither parent can unilaterally enroll the child in a new school, consent to non-emergency surgery, or baptize the child into a new faith without the other parent's agreement. When legal custody is sole, one parent holds that power alone.

Physical custody determines where the child lives and the daily schedule of time each parent spends with them. A parent with primary physical custody has the child the majority of overnights. Joint physical custody divides overnights more evenly, though an exact 50/50 split is neither required nor always appropriate.

The terms interact but operate independently. A father can hold joint legal custody—sharing every major decision—while having physical custody only on alternating weekends. Confusing the two leads to requests the court cannot grant and expectations the law does not support.

WHAT I'VE SEEN: The Decision That Wasn't Hers to Make

A mother with joint legal custody enrolled her eight-year-old in a private religious school without consulting the father. The father objected—not to the school's quality, but to the unilateral decision. The court agreed. Joint legal custody means joint decision-making, and the mother's failure to consult was treated as a violation of the custody order. The child was returned to public school. The mother was ordered to pay the father's attorney fees for the motion. And the judge noted the violation in the record—a credibility mark that followed her through the remainder of the case. One enrollment decision. Thousands of dollars. A stain on the record that colored every subsequent hearing.

The Best-Interest Standard

Every state applies some version of the "best interests of the child" test. The specific factors differ by jurisdiction, but the recurring themes are consistent:

- Each parent's ability to meet the child's daily physical, emotional, and developmental needs—who feeds, bathes, helps with homework, manages medical appointments, and maintains routines

- The quality and depth of each parent's relationship with the child—not just who the child "prefers," but who has been consistently present

- Emotional maturity—which parent demonstrates measured behavior under pressure and which escalates, rages, or collapses

- Safety—any history of abuse, neglect, domestic violence, substance impairment, or exposure to dangerous individuals

- Willingness to foster the child's relationship with the other parent—courts weigh this heavily, and the parent who obstructs or badmouths damages their own position

- The child's attachment to each parent, siblings, school, neighborhood, and community

- The child's own preferences, where age-appropriate and genuinely expressed—not coached, bribed, or pressured

- Each parent's physical and mental health, insofar as it affects parenting capacity

- Which parent is more likely to provide a stable, nurturing environment over the long term

Judges translate these factors into one practical question: which arrangement gives this child the best chance at a safe, stable, healthy life?

The Gravitational Force of the Status Quo

Among all the factors listed above, one exerts a pull that most parents underestimate until it is too late: the existing arrangement. Courts resist disrupting a routine that a child has adapted to—even if that routine was established by accident rather than design.

WHAT I'VE SEEN: The Apartment That Became the Answer

David and Karen separated in March. David moved into a two-bedroom apartment while the children—ages seven and ten—stayed with Karen in the family home. David assumed the arrangement was temporary. He planned to contest custody at trial eight months later. By the time trial arrived, the children had been living with Karen for most of the year. They were enrolled in a school near her home, settled into after-school activities, and sleeping in their own beds. David presented a strong case on the merits—he was an attentive father, the children adored him, and he held stable employment. The judge acknowledged all of it. Then the judge said: 'The children are settled. They are thriving in their current routine. I am not going to uproot them.' David received generous visitation. He did not receive primary custody. The decision had been made—not at trial, but eight months earlier, on the afternoon he moved out without a plan to preserve the status quo.

The lesson is direct: be deliberately intentional about the living arrangements and parenting routines you establish during separation. What you treat as temporary may become the framework the court refuses to alter.

Core Principle: *Whoever establishes the parenting pattern first often keeps it. The status quo is one of the most quietly powerful forces in custody law.*

The Three Custody Models

Cooperative Co-Parenting

Both parents communicate directly, share decision-making willingly, and accommodate reasonable schedule adjustments. This model requires mutual respect and a genuine ability to separate the failed marriage from current parenting. When it works, children benefit enormously, and courts reward the parents who sustain it.

Parallel Parenting

When direct communication produces conflict rather than resolution, parallel parenting minimizes contact between the adults while protecting each parent's relationship with the child. Communication is restricted to a monitored platform. Exchanges happen at neutral locations with no conversation beyond the handoff. Each parent governs their own household independently. A parenting coordinator resolves impasses.

Parallel parenting is not failure. It is the recognition that some combinations of personalities cannot co-parent safely—and that two separate islands of calm serve a child better than one interconnected battlefield.

Supervised Contact

When genuine safety concerns exist—active addiction, credible violence allegations, serious mental instability—the court may order one parent's time to occur under professional supervision. Supervision protects the child while preserving the parental bond. It is rarely permanent. A parent who completes treatment, maintains sobriety, or demonstrates sustained behavioral change may petition to move to unsupervised contact.

Age-Appropriate Scheduling

Infants and toddlers (0–3): Frequent, shorter contact with both parents. Attachment is built through repetition. Extended separations from a primary caregiver at this age produce anxiety and regression.

Overnights away from the primary attachment figure should be introduced gradually.

Preschool (3–5): Increasing tolerance for longer stretches. Overnights become feasible. Predictable routines—same pickup day, same bedtime, same morning ritual—matter more than total hours.

School-age (6–12): Longer blocks of uninterrupted time align with academic rhythms. Alternating weeks can work if both households provide structure. The school calendar should drive the schedule.

Teenagers (13+): Peer relationships, extracurricular commitments, and the drive for autonomy reshape everything. A rigid schedule that ignores a teenager's social world breeds resentment and resistance.

WHAT I'VE SEEN: The Schedule That Ignored the Child

A father insisted on strict alternating weeks with his fifteen-year-old daughter, including a provision that she could not attend weekend social events on 'his' time. The daughter—a straight-A student and varsity athlete with no behavioral issues—began refusing to go. The father filed a contempt motion against the mother for failing to enforce the schedule. The evaluator interviewed the daughter privately and concluded that her resistance was not alienation—it was the predictable response of a teenager whose autonomy was being disregarded by a parent who treated the schedule as more important than the relationship. The judge modified the arrangement to give the daughter more flexibility. The father's rigidity produced the opposite of what he intended: he ended up with less time, not more.

COMPANION VOLUME — For detailed age-specific scheduling templates, high-conflict parenting plan clauses, and advanced parallel parenting frameworks, see companion volume Chapters 17–18 and Appendix B.

CHAPTER 11

Protecting Your Children Through the Divorce

Children do not experience divorce the way adults do. They do not understand legal maneuvering or financial negotiation. What they register is the emotional temperature—the tension at dinner, the muffled arguing behind closed doors, the shift in a parent's voice when the phone buzzes, and the absence of the person who used to be there every morning.

The research is settled: children are damaged far less by the divorce itself than by the conflict surrounding it. A child whose parents separate but maintain civility and shield the child from hostility will generally adapt. A child trapped between warring parents—used as a messenger, interrogated after visits, burdened with adult rage—carries wounds that persist into adulthood.

How Children Absorb Conflict

A five-year-old does not need to hear the words of a hostile text to feel the parent's fury as they read it. A ten-year-old reads the tightened jaw at the exchange point and concludes, without asking, that something terrible is happening. A teenager who overhears one parent call the other a liar carries that phrase into their own understanding of what love and family mean.

Signs of stress in children during divorce:

- Stomachaches, headaches, or physical complaints without medical cause

- Sleep disturbance—nightmares, refusal to sleep alone, waking through the night

- Regression—bedwetting, thumb-sucking, clinginess in a child who had outgrown those behaviors

- Sudden academic decline or withdrawal from activities they previously loved

- Explosive anger or defiance that is completely out of character

- Emotional shutdown—retreating to their room, refusing to engage, going silent

- Hypervigilance—monitoring parental moods, trying to keep the peace, becoming the "perfect child"

- Self-blame—"If I had been better, this wouldn't have happened"

These are not behavioral problems. They are distress signals. If you are seeing them, your child is telling you something in the only language available to them.

The Bright Lines You Must Not Cross

- Discussing the case, hearings, filings, legal strategy, or money disputes with your child—at any age

- Using your child as a messenger: "Tell your father I need the check by Friday"

- Interrogating them about the other parent's home, dating life, spending, or conduct

- Criticizing your spouse within your child's hearing—a wider radius than you imagine
- Crying, venting, or displaying visible distress that burdens them with your pain
- Enlisting them as an ally or emotional support: "You're the only one who understands"
- Allowing extended family to disparage the other parent in your child's presence
- Posting about your child's struggles, therapy, or custody distress on social media
- Asking your child where they want to live—a decision no child should carry
- Monitoring their communications with the other parent

WHAT I'VE SEEN: The Mother Who Became the Conflict

Sandra believed she was protecting her nine-year-old son, Michael, by keeping him informed. After each hearing, she sat him down and explained what happened. She described what his father's attorney had argued. She showed him text messages she found objectionable, saying, 'I want you to see who he really is.' Michael began having panic attacks before exchanges. His grades dropped two letter grades in one semester. His therapist reported that the boy was consumed with worry about 'what's happening in court'—information no nine-year-old should possess. The custody evaluator identified Sandra as the primary source of Michael's distress. Not the father. Sandra. She was a loving mother who had convinced herself that honesty meant transparency. It did not. What she called transparency was exposure to adult conflict disguised as parenting, and it cost her the presumption she walked in with: that she was the more protective parent.

When the Other Parent Pulls the Children In

If your spouse is badmouthing you, pumping the children for information, coaching their statements, or engineering loyalty conflicts—your instinct will scream at you to set the record straight. To tell your side. To make sure your child knows the truth.

Do not.

Retaliating by engaging the child in the same behavior eliminates the distinction between you and the person doing it. Two parents pulling a child in opposite directions is not a tie. It is mutual destruction—and evaluators classify it as exactly that.

Instead:

- Document what the child reports—factually, without leading questions, using the log template in Chapter 47

- Do not ask: "Did Daddy say something mean about me?" Ask: "How was your weekend?"

- Consult your attorney about whether the pattern warrants intervention

- Continue being the parent who shields. Over time, that contrast decides cases.

Talking to Your Children About the Divorce

Ages 3–6: "Mommy and Daddy are going to live in two different houses now. You did absolutely nothing wrong. We both love you so much, and that will never, ever change."

Ages 7–12: "We've decided to live apart. I know that's hard to hear. It's okay to feel sad, confused, or angry. This is a decision between adults. It is not your fault. Both of your parents love you completely."

Ages 13+: "I want to be honest about what's happening, and I want to protect you from details that belong between adults. The marriage is ending. You don't need to take sides. Your relationship with each of us is yours."

Supporting a Distressed Child Without Interrogating

When your child returns from the other household visibly upset, the temptation to question them is overwhelming. What they need is comfort, not a deposition.

- Stay calm. Your nervous system sets the tone for theirs.

- Offer connection: "You're safe. I'm right here."

- Use open-ended questions if they want to talk: "How did things feel today?"

- Never ask loaded questions: "Was Dad drinking again?" "Did Mom's boyfriend yell at you?"

- If they volunteer information, listen without visible reaction—no gasping, no rage, no "I knew it."

- Record their exact words in your log afterward, using their language, not your interpretation.

- Ask what they need. Sometimes a hug and a normal evening are more healing than any conversation.

The Three-Level Response to Concerns

Level 1: Document Only

Poor judgment that is not dangerous: inconsistent routines, excessive screen time, junk food, minor schedule violations. Record it. Do not confront. Flag patterns for your attorney.

Level 2: Document and Consult Professionals

The child reports fear or escalating anxiety. Repeated exposure to intense conflict. Suspected substance use. Noticeable behavioral shifts after visits. A new partner who raises concerns. Record everything, stay calm, and consult the child's therapist, pediatrician, school counselor, or your attorney.

Level 3: Immediate Action

Intoxicated caregiving. Violence or credible threats. Abandonment. A child left in an unsafe environment. Active criminal behavior with the child present. Contact law enforcement if necessary. Document everything. Notify your attorney immediately. Even in emergencies, factual steadiness protects your position.

> **Core Principle:** *Your child is not a participant in this case. They are the reason for it. Every action you take should widen the distance between your child and the conflict—never narrow it.*

COMPANION VOLUME — For the complete child protection guide in high-conflict custody—including alienation recognition, therapeutic intervention, and age-specific scripts—see companion volume Chapters 5–9 and 12.

CHAPTER 12

Custody Evaluations, GALs, and Court-Appointed Experts

At some point in a contested custody case, a professional will enter the picture whose opinion may outweigh everything else in the file. A custody evaluator. A guardian ad litem. A court-appointed psychologist. Their report or recommendation can redirect the trajectory of the case in ways that months of attorney argument cannot.

Understanding who these professionals are, what they look for, and how to present yourself to them is the preparation that frequently determines the outcome.

What a Custody Evaluation Involves

A custody evaluation is an independent assessment conducted by a licensed mental health professional—typically a psychologist or clinical social worker with forensic specialization. The evaluator gathers information from every available source, assesses each parent and the child, and delivers a written report containing findings and recommendations.

The process typically spans weeks to months and includes:

- Individual interviews with each parent, often across multiple sessions

- Observation of each parent interacting with the child—at the evaluator's office, during home visits, or both

- Home visits to each household to observe the child's living environment

- Psychological testing—personality inventories, parenting assessments, and sometimes cognitive screenings

- Collateral contacts—interviews with teachers, therapists, pediatricians, neighbors, coaches, and daycare providers

- Review of court documents, police reports, medical records, school records, and communication logs

The resulting report—often thirty to sixty pages—frequently becomes the single most influential document in the case. Judges give evaluator recommendations substantial weight because the evaluator has spent dozens of hours with the family, observing dynamics the judge will never witness.

WHAT I'VE SEEN: The Father Who Prepared and the Father Who Performed

---

Two fathers in separate cases faced evaluations within the same year, both before the same evaluator. The first arrived with organized documentation: a timeline of his parenting involvement, his child's school and medical records with his attendance noted, communication logs showing calm BIFF responses, and a brief written summary of his concerns. When asked about the mother, he said: 'She's a capable mother in many ways. My concern is specific—her new partner has a documented history of violence, and I've observed changes in my daughter's behavior since he moved into the home.' The evaluator noted his specificity, his restraint, and his willingness to acknowledge the mother's strengths. The second father arrived with a speech. He spent forty minutes cataloguing every wrong his ex-wife had committed since 2016. He could not name a single positive quality she possessed as a parent. When the evaluator redirected him to discuss his own parenting, he returned to his grievances within two sentences. The report noted that the second father 'appeared more focused on the litigation than on his child's daily experience.' Same evaluator. Same process. Radically different outcomes based on how each man showed up.

How to Present Yourself

Evaluators have observed thousands of parents. They detect rehearsed performances and exaggeration with surgical precision. What earns their trust:

- Answer questions directly. Do not deflect, monologue, or pivot every response toward your spouse's failings.

- Acknowledge imperfections. "I lost my temper on that occasion and I regret it. Here is what I've done since then to manage my reactions" builds trust. "I have never made a mistake as a parent" invites skepticism.

- Describe concerns in factual, behavioral terms. "On three documented dates, the children were returned without dinner having been prepared, homework was incomplete, and my daughter reported that her father was asleep when she arrived home from school" is credible. "He's a neglectful father" is dismissible.

- Demonstrate genuine involvement. Describe homework routines, bedtime rituals, favorite meals you prepare, medical appointments you manage, and how you handle behavioral challenges.

- Keep your home natural. Evaluators see through staged perfection. A clean, functional, child-friendly household communicates stability. A museum-quality display communicates performance.

- Show—rather than claim—support for the other parent's relationship with the child. "I keep photos of their mother in their bedroom" or "I always encourage them to call their dad before bed" resonates more than abstract assertions about co-parenting.

Guardians Ad Litem

A guardian ad litem—abbreviated GAL—is an attorney or trained professional appointed to represent the child's interests. The GAL's client is the child, not either parent. This distinction gives their opinion outsized influence with judges. The GAL investigates independently: interviewing witnesses, reviewing records, visiting homes, attending hearings, and sometimes testifying directly.

Treat every interaction with the GAL the same way you would treat testimony under oath—honest, organized, measured, and focused entirely on what your child needs.

Red Flags Evaluators and GALs Watch For

- A parent who cannot identify a single positive quality in the other parent

- A narrative built entirely on blame with zero self-reflection

- A child who uses adult language or legal terms to describe a parent—"My dad has narcissistic personality disorder" from an eight-year-old signals coaching

- Gaps between what a parent tells the evaluator and what the records show

- A parent who appears more invested in winning than in the child's actual experience

- Attempts to control the evaluator's access to information or witnesses

- A home environment that looks staged rather than lived-in—or one in which the child's space appears neglected

Green Lights That Strengthen Your Position

- A parent who acknowledges the child's need for both parents—even when the other parent makes that difficult

- Documentation presented calmly, in organized form, without editorial commentary

- Engagement with therapy, parenting classes, or support that demonstrates growth and self-awareness

- A child who appears relaxed, comfortable, and age-appropriately connected during observed interactions

- A parent who asks: "What can I do to support my child through this?" rather than "How do I prove my ex is unfit?"

WHAT I'VE SEEN: The Home Visit That Spoke Volumes

The evaluator visited two households in one week. In the first home, the children's bedrooms had personalized spaces—artwork on the walls that the children had clearly made themselves, books on shelves matched to each child's reading level, a homework station with supplies, and framed photos of both parents. The refrigerator held meal-prepped containers labeled with each child's name. In the second home, the children's room contained a bed, a bare desk, and a television. No personal items. No photos. No evidence that the children spent meaningful time there. The evaluator's report did not use the word 'neglect.' It used the phrase 'limited evidence of child-centered living space.' That phrase carried weight. The first parent received primary custody. The evidence was not dramatic—it was domestic.

Refrigerator labels and crayon drawings. But it painted a picture of which household revolved around the children and which household treated them as visitors.

Core Principle: *Every interaction with an evaluator or GAL is an audition for custody. They are watching how you discuss your child, how you discuss your spouse, and whether the gap between those two reveals a protector or a combatant.*

COMPANION VOLUME — For the complete custody evaluation preparation guide—home visit checklists, psychological testing expectations, and strategies for working with GALs and parenting coordinators—see companion volume Chapter 16.

CHAPTER 13

Parenting Plans and Schedules That Judges Trust

A parenting plan is the operating manual for your child's life after divorce. Done well, it prevents conflict by replacing ambiguity with structure. Done poorly, it becomes the single largest generator of post-judgment motions, emergency hearings, and attorney fees in family law.

The difference between a plan that works and one that fails is specificity. Every vague sentence is a fault line waiting for pressure. Every undefined term is an invitation for a high-conflict spouse to exploit.

WHAT I'VE SEEN: The Word That Cost $14,000

A parenting plan stated that the father would have the children "during the Christmas holiday." Nothing else. No start date. No end date. No clarification of whether "Christmas" meant Christmas Eve, Christmas Day, or the entire winter break. In December, the father arrived on the 20th, asserting the holiday began with school dismissal. The mother refused, insisting the holiday meant December 25th only. A motion was filed. An emergency hearing followed. Attorneys billed on both sides. Total cost: approximately $14,000. The judge ultimately defined "Christmas holiday" as December 24th at 6:00 PM through December 26th at 6:00 PM and ordered the *attorneys to redraft the entire holiday schedule in exhaustive detail. One undefined word. Fourteen thousand dollars. Two children who spent the week before Christmas watching their parents fight in a courtroom.*

What a Strong Parenting Plan Contains

The Regular Schedule

Specify which parent has the child on which days and overnights. Name the days. State pickup and drop-off times to the hour. "Alternating weekends" is not specific enough. "Parent B's weekend begins Friday at 6:00 PM and ends Sunday at 6:00 PM, alternating on an odd/even week basis beginning with Week 1 of the calendar year" eliminates argument.

Holiday and School Break Schedule

Assign every major holiday and school break to a specific parent in a specific year, with alternation in subsequent years. Define start and end times precisely. Cover Thanksgiving, Christmas Eve, Christmas Day, New Year's Eve, New Year's Day, Easter or Passover, spring break, summer break, Mother's Day, Father's Day, each parent's birthday, each child's birthday, Halloween, and any culturally significant dates. State that holiday schedules override the regular rotation and that there is no "make-up" time unless explicitly provided.

Summer and Vacation Time

How are extended breaks divided? How far in advance must a parent notify the other of travel plans—typically thirty to sixty days? Can travel include international destinations? Is written consent required for out-of-state travel? What are the consequences if notice is not provided?

Decision-Making Authority

Assign tie-breaking authority when joint legal custodians disagree: Mother decides medical issues, Father decides education, or all disputes go through a parenting coordinator. The phrase "the parties shall consult and agree" means nothing without a mechanism for resolving the inevitable moment when they do not agree.

Right of First Refusal

If the custodial parent cannot be with the child for a defined period—commonly four or more hours—the other parent is offered the time before a babysitter is called. This prevents situations where a child spends the weekend with a sitter while the other parent sits available and willing at home.

Communication Protocols

Name the platform (OurFamilyWizard, TalkingParents, email only). Set response expectations—twenty-four hours for non-emergencies. Prohibit communication through the child. Specify whether the child has phone or video access to the non-residential parent during the other's time, and at what hours.

Exchange Procedures

In high-conflict cases: a neutral public location, a specified time, no conversation beyond the handoff, and no uninvited third parties. State who walks the child in and who drives away first, if that level of detail prevents conflict. For some families, it does.

Substance Use Provisions

Testing requirements (Soberlink, hair follicle, random urine analysis). Sobriety obligations during parenting time and for a defined window before. Consequences for a positive test or refusal to test—automatic suspension of overnights, mandatory evaluation, or return to supervised contact.

New Partner and Overnight Guest Provisions

A minimum relationship duration—often three to six months—before introducing a new partner to the child. Restrictions on unrelated overnight guests when the child is present. Notification requirements.

Relocation Restrictions

Advance notice of sixty to ninety days before either parent can move. A definition of relocation—beyond a specific mileage radius, outside the school district, or out of state. The other parent's right to contest and the process for doing so.

Schedule Structures Courts Favor

Alternating weeks: One week with each parent, rotating on a set day. Works well for school-age children when both parents live near the school. Minimizes transitions while maximizing time with each parent.

5-2-2-5: Parent A always has Monday–Tuesday, Parent B always has Wednesday–Thursday, weekends alternate Friday through Sunday. A consistent weekday pattern that young school-age children adapt to quickly because they always know whose house they're waking up in on a school morning.

Every-other-weekend plus midweek: One parent has primary custody. The other receives alternating weekends and one midweek overnight. Common when one parent has been the historical primary caregiver.

2-2-3 rotation: Two days Parent A, two days Parent B, three-day weekend alternates. No parent goes longer than three days without seeing the child. Suited to younger children who benefit from frequent contact with both households.

Provisions That Prevent Future Litigation

- Mediation-first clause: disputes go to a mediator before either parent files a motion

- Parenting coordinator provision: a designated professional makes binding decisions on day-to-day disputes

- Schedule violation penalties: if a parent is more than thirty minutes late without notice, the other parent's time is extended by an equivalent period

- Communication blackout: no discussion of litigation, legal strategy, or the other parent's perceived failings during exchanges or in the child's presence

- Annual review clause: the schedule is revisited as the child's developmental needs evolve, without requiring formal modification proceedings

- Transportation cost-sharing formula: specified in writing to prevent quarterly disputes over gas money

- Technology provisions: which parent provides the child's phone, what monitoring is permitted, and whether location sharing is enabled between households

---

WHAT I'VE SEEN: The Plan That Paid for Itself

Rachel and Tom's attorney spent three additional hours drafting a parenting plan that addressed twenty-two specific contingencies—holiday definitions down to the hour, a three-tier dispute resolution process, Soberlink monitoring provisions, right of first refusal, new *partner introduction timelines, and a relocation consent clause. The additional drafting cost: approximately $1,200. In the three years following the divorce, Rachel and Tom returned to court zero times. A colleague's clients—with a two-page boilerplate plan from the same courthouse—returned six times over the same period, spending a combined $38,000 in legal fees on disputes that a thorough plan would have prevented. One plan cost $1,200 upfront and produced three years of quiet compliance. The other cost nothing extra upfront and produced $38,000 in avoidable conflict. The math speaks for itself.*

Core Principle: *A detailed parenting plan is not a sign of distrust. It is a recognition that clarity prevents conflict—and that your child's daily life depends on a framework strong enough to survive whatever the adults put it through.*

COMPANION VOLUME — For the complete parenting plan template library—including high-conflict provisions, holiday rotation samples, substance abuse safeguards, and relocation clauses—see companion volume Chapters 17–18 and Appendix B.

Financial accuracy and disciplined compliance protect your position on both sides of the support calculation.

PART IV

CHILD SUPPORT AND INCIDENTAL EXPENSES

Money and children intersect at one of the most emotionally charged points in divorce. Child support is not alimony by another name. It is not a reward for the custodial parent or a punishment for the non-custodial one. It is a legal obligation rooted in a simple premise: both parents bear financial responsibility for the children they brought into the world, and the law provides mechanisms to ensure that responsibility is met.

The three chapters ahead cover how support is calculated, what happens with the incidental expenses that no guideline formula anticipates, and what tools exist when an obligation is ignored or when circumstances change enough to justify a different number.

CHAPTER 14

Child Support — Calculation, Negotiation, and Protection

Child support generates more confusion, resentment, and misinformation per dollar than any other financial issue in divorce. Paying parents feel exploited. Receiving parents feel shortchanged. Both sides operate with incomplete information about how the numbers are actually derived, what the law permits, and where the real disputes lie.

Cutting through that confusion starts here.

What Child Support Covers

At its core, child support addresses the baseline costs of raising a child: housing, food, clothing, transportation, basic medical care, and the routine expenses of daily life. It is calculated to ensure that children experience a standard of living reasonably consistent with what both parents can collectively provide—not to enrich or impoverish either household.

Child support does not typically cover extraordinary expenses—private school tuition, braces, specialized therapy, competitive sports fees, or college costs. Those fall into a separate category addressed in Chapter 15.

The Two Dominant Calculation Models

Income Shares

The majority of states use an income-shares model. Both parents' gross incomes are combined to determine the total financial resources available to the child. A table or formula—published in the state's child support guidelines—establishes the total support obligation for a family at that income level with that number of children. Each parent's share is then proportional to their percentage of the combined income.

If Parent A earns $80,000 and Parent B earns $40,000, the combined income is $120,000. Parent A contributes roughly 67 percent and Parent B roughly 33 percent. The guideline table specifies what a family at that income level should spend on children. Each parent pays their proportional share—with credits and adjustments for the custodial arrangement, health insurance premiums, and childcare costs.

Percentage of Income

A smaller number of states use a percentage-of-income model, where the noncustodial parent pays a flat percentage of their gross or net income—typically ranging from 17 to 25 percent for one child, with incremental increases for additional children. The custodial parent's income may or may not factor into the calculation, depending on the state.

Neither model is inherently fairer. Both produce results that feel wrong to someone. The purpose of guidelines is not perfect equity—it is consistency. Courts want similarly situated families to receive similar outcomes rather than results that hinge on which judge happened to hear the case.

✦ ✦ ✦

Defining Income: Where the Fights Begin

The most contentious element of any child support calculation is not the formula—it is the number fed into the formula. How "income" is defined determines everything.

Gross vs. net. Most states use gross income as the starting point—wages, salaries, commissions, bonuses, overtime, tips, investment returns, rental income, trust distributions, and sometimes even non-cash benefits like employer-provided housing or a company vehicle. Mandatory deductions (taxes, Social Security, Medicare, mandatory retirement contributions, union dues) are subtracted in some states to arrive at an adjusted figure.

Bonuses and commissions. If a significant portion of income is variable—annual bonuses, sales commissions, seasonal overtime—courts typically average those payments over two to three years to prevent gaming. A parent who "happens" to have a low-bonus year during the support calculation period invites judicial skepticism.

Self-employment income. This is where child support disputes become forensic exercises. A parent who owns a business controls what appears on the tax return. Personal expenses routed through the company—a vehicle, meals, travel, a cell phone, home office deductions—reduce reported income without reducing actual spending power. Courts and forensic accountants look past the tax return to the lifestyle the income supports. If a parent reports $60,000 in income but lives in a $500,000 home, drives a new SUV, and vacations internationally, the court will want to understand the gap.

Investment and passive income. Dividends, rental proceeds, capital gains, royalties, trust distributions—all of these can be included in the income calculation. Wealthy parents who structure income to minimize reported earnings face increasing judicial sophistication about these techniques.

◆ ◆ ◆

Imputed Income: When the Court Assigns What You Could Earn

A parent who voluntarily reduces their earning capacity—quitting a well-paying job to work part-time, declining a promotion, retiring early without medical necessity, or simply choosing not to work—may find the court unimpressed. Courts have the authority to impute income: assigning an earning figure based on the parent's education, work history, skills, and the local job market rather than what they are actually earning.

Imputation cuts both ways. A paying parent who reduces income to lower support faces imputation. A receiving parent who refuses to seek employment when capable of working may also face imputation—reducing the support they receive.

The triggering question is whether the reduction in income is voluntary or involuntary. A parent laid off during an industry downturn has an involuntary reduction. A parent who quits to "find themselves" after separation does not. The distinction is factual and case-specific, but the judicial suspicion attached to conveniently timed income reductions is universal.

WHAT I'VE SEEN: One Photo, Eighteen Months

The weekend after a favorable temporary hearing, Vanessa posted on Instagram. She was at a rooftop bar with a man the children hadn't met, holding champagne, with the caption: 'New chapter. New me. #blessed.' Her schedule showed the children were with her that weekend. The husband's attorney enlarged the photograph to *poster size and mounted it on an easel at the next hearing. Three questions: Was this taken during your parenting time? Who is this man? Have the children met him? The judge noted the photo raised questions about 'the prioritization of social activity over parenting responsibility and the premature introduction of romantic partners.' Vanessa lost primary custody at the temporary stage. Eighteen months, a full evaluation, and $31,000 in additional fees to regain it. One photograph. One caption. One moment of celebration that a judge interpreted as evidence of misplaced priorities.*

How Custody Arrangements Affect the Calculation

The allocation of overnight stays between households directly affects child support in most states. A parent with more overnights incurs greater direct expenses—housing, food, utilities, transportation. Support formulas typically account for this by reducing the non-custodial parent's obligation as their overnight percentage increases.

In shared custody arrangements where overnights approach an even split, the support obligation may shrink significantly or, in some states, be offset entirely—with only the difference between each parent's proportional share being paid by the higher earner. This creates a financial incentive to seek more parenting time that courts monitor carefully. A parent who suddenly demands additional overnights during a support proceeding without any prior history of pursuing extra time invites the inference that the motivation is financial rather than parental.

Deviation Factors

Guideline amounts are presumptive, not absolute. Courts retain discretion to deviate upward or downward based on specific circumstances:

- A child with extraordinary medical, educational, or developmental needs

- Significant travel expenses for long-distance visitation

- A parent's obligation to support children from another relationship

- Substantial assets available to either parent beyond earned income

- A child's independent income or resources (trusts, inheritance)

- Shared custody arrangements that are not captured well by the formula

- The standard of living the child would have enjoyed had the family remained intact

Requesting a deviation requires evidence—not merely an assertion that the guideline result feels wrong. Document the specific circumstances that justify the departure and present them clearly.

Tax Treatment After 2017

Prior to the Tax Cuts and Jobs Act of 2017, child support was tax-neutral—neither deductible by the payer nor taxable to the recipient. That remains unchanged. However, the Act eliminated the dependency exemption for children, replacing it with an increased child tax credit. The question of which parent claims the child for tax purposes—and the associated credits—has become a frequent settlement negotiation point. Ensure your agreement addresses this explicitly. Ambiguity here generates post-judgment disputes that cost more in attorney fees than the credit itself is worth.

The Importance of Accurate Financial Disclosure

Every child support proceeding requires financial disclosure—typically through sworn income and expense declarations. Understating income, omitting assets, inflating expenses, or misrepresenting financial circumstances on a sworn document is perjury. Courts treat financial dishonesty in support proceedings with particular severity because the harmed party is, ultimately, the child.

If your spouse's financial disclosure appears inaccurate, discovery tools exist to investigate. If your own financial picture is complicated, present it transparently and let your attorney frame it favorably rather than concealing information that will eventually surface.

Core Principle: *Child support exists for your children's needs—not as leverage, punishment, or reward. Courts respond harshly when either parent manipulates the process. Honesty about income is not a concession. It is the price of credibility.*

CHAPTER 15

Incidental Child Expenses — The Disputes Nobody Warns You About

Child support guidelines address baseline needs. They do not address the orthodontist who recommends braces at $6,000. They do not cover the travel soccer league that costs $4,500 per season. They are silent on whether the child should attend public school or the private academy one parent insists upon. They say nothing about the therapist both parents agree the child needs but neither wants to pay for.

These incidental expenses generate more post-judgment disputes than almost any other issue in family law—not because the amounts are large in isolation, but because every receipt becomes a referendum on values, priorities, and control. Getting the framework right during the divorce saves years of conflict after it.

Medical, Dental, and Mental Health Expenses

Most agreements distinguish between "covered" and "extraordinary" medical expenses. Routine care covered by insurance—annual physicals, dental cleanings, standard prescriptions—is absorbed within the base support obligation. Extraordinary expenses—those not covered by insurance or that exceed a defined threshold—are typically split between parents, either equally or in proportion to income.

The disputes arise at the boundary. Is orthodontia routine or extraordinary? What about a therapist at $200 per session? Vision correction surgery for a teenager? Allergy treatment that insurance covers partially? Define these categories in your agreement with as much specificity as possible. Include a dollar threshold below which expenses are absorbed by the incurring parent and above which they trigger the sharing obligation.

Health insurance coverage should be addressed explicitly: which parent carries the policy, how premiums are allocated, what happens if employer-provided coverage is lost, and whether COBRA continuation is required during a transition period.

Extracurricular Activities

The travel baseball team, the dance studio, the coding camp, the music lessons, the summer enrichment program—these expenses accumulate with startling speed, and they sit at the intersection of every parent's desire to give their child opportunities and every co-parent's concern about being committed to costs they did not agree to.

A well-drafted agreement addresses whether both parents must consent before a child is enrolled in an activity that exceeds a specified cost, how costs are divided for activities both parents support, what happens when one parent unilaterally enrolls the child in an expensive program, and whether existing activities at the time of divorce are treated differently from new ones.

Without these provisions, a parent who enrolls the child in a $5,000-per-year activity and then demands that the other parent cover half has created a dispute the court may need to resolve—at a cost that frequently exceeds the activity fee itself.

WHAT I'VE SEEN: The Business That Shrank on Paper

Warren's landscaping company had generated $220,000 in gross revenue annually for five years. In the year the support calculation was pending, his reported income dropped to $74,000. He had restructured the business, routing payments through a new entity registered to his girlfriend's mother. Trucks were transferred to the girlfriend's name. Employees were reclassified as independent contractors paid through the new entity. The forensic accountant traced every payment, cross-referenced client invoices with deposits across all three entities, and reconstructed Warren's actual cash flow at $207,000. The court imputed income at the five-year average, imposed sanctions for fraudulent disclosure, and ordered Warren to pay the $14,000 forensic analysis fee. His attempt to lower support produced the opposite: higher imputed income, sanctions, and a credibility collapse that infected every other issue in the case.

◆ ◆ ◆

Childcare and Daycare

Work-related childcare expenses are typically shared in proportion to income. The key disputes involve whether the expense is genuinely work-related (a parent claiming childcare costs while attending school full-time faces scrutiny), whether the provider is reasonable in cost (a luxury nanny service versus a licensed daycare center), and whether the need continues as the child ages (a twelve-year-old may not require the same after-school care as a six-year-old).

Document the necessity, the cost, and the connection to employment. Include provisions for notice and verification—the paying parent should receive receipts or invoices demonstrating that the expense was actually incurred.

Private School and College Contributions

Whether a court can order a parent to contribute to private school tuition or college expenses varies dramatically by state. Some jurisdictions treat education as a parental obligation that extends through college. Others hold that once a child reaches the age of majority, the financial obligation ends.

If both parents attended private school or college, if the child was enrolled in private school during the marriage, or if the child has educational needs that a public school cannot adequately address, courts are more likely to order continued contribution. The time to negotiate these provisions is during the divorce—not when the acceptance letter arrives and the tuition bill follows.

College contribution clauses should specify the maximum annual amount, whether the obligation is limited to in-state public university rates, what the child's own financial responsibilities are (scholarships, part-time employment, student loans), and whether the contribution is conditioned on academic performance or the child maintaining a relationship with the paying parent.

Drafting Expense Provisions That Prevent Future Conflict

The most effective incidental expense clauses share common characteristics:

- A clear dollar threshold distinguishing routine from extraordinary expenses
- A defined allocation method (50/50, pro rata by income, or a fixed formula)
- A notice requirement: the parent proposing the expense must provide written notice and a specified period for the other parent to object

- An approval mechanism: expenses above a defined amount require mutual consent before the obligation attaches

- A reimbursement timeline: the contributing parent pays within thirty days of receiving documentation

- A dispute resolution provision: if the parents disagree about an expense, they submit it to a mediator or parenting coordinator before filing a motion

Core Principle: *The best time to negotiate incidental expense terms is during the divorce—when both sides have attorneys, when the court is available to resolve disputes, and when the cost of getting it right is a fraction of the cost of getting it wrong.*

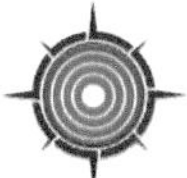

Enforcing and Modifying Child Support

A child support order is only as valuable as the willingness—or compulsion—to honor it. When the obligor stops paying, the consequences ripple through the receiving household in ways the court never intended. When circumstances change substantially enough that the existing order no longer fits reality, the law provides mechanisms to adjust. Understanding both enforcement and modification protects you regardless of which side of the obligation you occupy.

When a Parent Refuses to Pay

Nonpayment of child support is not a civil disagreement. It is a violation of a court order, and courts possess a formidable arsenal of enforcement tools:

Contempt of court. The most common enforcement mechanism. The receiving parent files a motion alleging that the paying parent has willfully failed to comply with the order. If the court finds contempt, the consequences range from fines to incarceration—and the unpaid balance does not disappear. Arrearages accumulate, often with interest.

Income withholding orders. Courts can direct the obligor's employer to withhold the support amount directly from wages before the paycheck reaches the parent. This eliminates the "I forgot" defense and is the single most effective collection tool available. In many states, income withholding is automatic upon entry of the support order.

Tax refund interception. Federal and state tax refunds can be intercepted and applied to child support arrearages. The IRS and state revenue agencies participate in offset programs that redirect refunds to the custodial parent or state disbursement unit.

License suspension. Driver's licenses, professional licenses (medical, legal, real estate, contractor), and recreational licenses (hunting, fishing) can be suspended for persistent nonpayment. Passport denial is available for arrearages exceeding a statutory threshold—currently $2,500 at the federal level.

Liens and asset seizure. Courts can place liens on real property, bank accounts, investment accounts, and other assets owned by the delinquent parent. In extreme cases, the assets can be seized and liquidated to satisfy the debt.

Credit reporting. Child support arrearages are reportable to credit bureaus. A delinquent parent's credit score—and their ability to obtain mortgages, car loans, and credit cards—can be materially damaged.

State child support enforcement agencies (typically within the Department of Social Services or a similar body) can pursue many of these remedies without requiring the receiving parent to hire an attorney. If you are owed support and the obligor has stopped paying, contact your state's enforcement office as a first step.

Modification: When Circumstances Change

Child support orders are not permanent in the way property division is. They are modifiable when a material change in circumstances has occurred since the order was entered. The threshold varies by state, but the principle is consistent: the change must be substantial, involuntary, and ongoing—not temporary, self-created, or speculative.

Common Grounds for Modification

- Significant involuntary income change: job loss, disability, industry downturn, company closure
- Significant income increase by either parent
- A change in the custodial arrangement (more or fewer overnights)
- A child's evolving needs: new medical conditions, educational requirements, therapeutic needs
- Remarriage or new children (in some jurisdictions, though courts are increasingly skeptical of reducing support to earlier children based on voluntary decisions to expand a family)
- Emancipation of one child in a multi-child order, requiring recalculation
- A change in health insurance availability or cost

The Self-Protection Imperative for Paying Parents

If you are the obligor and your circumstances have changed—you lost your job, your business contracted, your health deteriorated—file for modification immediately. Do not wait. Do not simply stop paying and assume the court will eventually understand. Arrearages accumulate from the date of the existing order, not from the date you file for modification. Every month you delay is a month of debt at the full original amount that you may never be able to discharge.

Child support arrearages cannot be discharged in bankruptcy. They survive death in many jurisdictions, becoming claims against the estate. The obligation does not go away because you ignored it. File for modification the moment the change occurs, support the filing with evidence (termination letter, medical records, financial statements), and continue paying whatever you can while the modification is pending. Courts treat a parent who demonstrates good faith—paying something, communicating with the enforcement agency, filing promptly—far more favorably than one who disappears.

Modification Strategy for Receiving Parents

If you believe the paying parent's income has increased materially since the original order—a promotion, a new business, an inheritance, a dramatic lifestyle upgrade—you may have grounds to seek an upward modification. The evidence required mirrors what you would present in the initial calculation: tax returns, pay stubs, business records, lifestyle indicators, and any public information suggesting a change in financial circumstances.

Timing matters. Some states impose a minimum waiting period between modification requests. Others require a minimum percentage change in the guideline amount before a modification will be considered. Consult your attorney about the specific procedural requirements before filing.

Arrearages: What Accumulates and What Cannot Be Forgiven

Unpaid child support accumulates as arrearages. In most states, arrearages accrue interest—sometimes at rates significantly above market. The total owed can escalate rapidly when a parent falls behind and does not seek timely modification.

Courts have limited authority to forgive arrearages retroactively. The general rule is that past-due support is vested in the child (or the custodial parent who fronted the expenses) and cannot be waived by the court without the consent of the party to whom it is owed. Even agreements between parents to "forgive" arrearages may not be enforceable if the state's enforcement agency is involved.

The lesson is stark: if you owe support and cannot pay the full amount, do not default silently. File for modification. Pay what you can. Communicate with the enforcement agency. Document your efforts. A parent who demonstrates good faith in the face of hardship receives judicial sympathy. A parent who vanishes receives warrants.

WHAT I'VE SEEN: Fourteen Months of Silence

Ray lost his sales management position when his company downsized in January. His support obligation was $2,800 monthly based on $125,000 annual salary. Embarrassed and certain he would find comparable work quickly, Ray stopped paying in February and told no one. By July, he had taken a warehouse job at $42,000. He still did not file for modification. In November of the following year—fourteen months after the job loss—his ex-wife filed contempt. Arrears had accumulated to $39,200. Interest added $3,400. Ray's attorney filed for modification, but the court could only modify prospectively from the filing date. Fourteen months of arrears at the original amount were locked in. Ray was ordered to repay the full arrearage at $600 monthly on top of his reduced obligation. It took three and a half years. A colleague laid off from the same company the same month filed for modification within two weeks. His obligation was reduced within sixty days. Zero arrears accumulated. Same layoff. Same hardship. One man filed promptly. The other waited. That single decision created a $42,600 difference.

> **Core Principle:** *Child support orders are enforceable, modifiable, and survivable across virtually every circumstance. If you are owed money, the law provides tools. If you cannot pay, the law provides a path to adjustment. What the law does not provide is patience for parents who ignore their obligations and hope the problem resolves itself.*

WHAT I'VE SEEN: The $3,200 Program That Cost $12,000

Nine-year-old Lily had studied violin for three years and showed genuine talent. Her mother enrolled her in a competitive youth orchestra costing $3,200 per season without consulting the father. He refused to pay—not because he opposed music, but because the decision was unilateral. The mother filed to compel contribution. The father cross-moved, arguing the enrollment violated their agreement's mutual consent requirement for expenses over $500. Both attorneys prepared briefs and attended a hearing. Combined fees: $12,400. The judge ruled the mother had violated the consent provision and could not compel contribution—but removing Lily from a program she loved would harm the child. Lily continued at the mother's sole expense. Lily, who overheard her parents arguing in the courthouse hallway, told her therapist the following week that she wanted to quit violin because 'it makes everyone fight.' The program survived. The joy did not.

Alimony outcomes depend on credible presentation of need or ability to pay—supported by financial documentation, not emotional argument.

PART V

SPOUSAL SUPPORT AND ALIMONY

Spousal support provokes more raw emotion per dollar than any other issue in divorce. The paying spouse sees it as punishment for a marriage that failed. The receiving spouse sees it as the bare minimum required to survive the economic devastation that divorce often inflicts on the lower-earning partner. Both are wrong—and both are partially right.

Alimony is neither a reward nor a penalty. It is a financial mechanism designed to address the economic imbalance created when one spouse sacrificed earning capacity for the benefit of the marriage—raising children, supporting a career, maintaining a household—while the other spouse's income and professional trajectory grew. The three chapters ahead explain how courts analyze support, how to position yourself on either side of the equation, and what happens when circumstances change after the order is entered.

CHAPTER 17

Spousal Support — What It Is, Who Receives It, and Why

In 1985, a spouse who had stayed home for twenty years to raise children could expect permanent alimony as a near-certainty. The social contract was understood: one partner earned, one partner maintained the home, and if the marriage ended, the earning partner continued to provide. That world has largely vanished. Modern alimony law reflects a society that expects both adults to work toward self-sufficiency—while still recognizing that marriages create economic dependencies that cannot be unwound overnight.

Understanding where the law stands today—not where it stood a generation ago, and not where popular culture imagines it to be—is the first step toward protecting yourself whether you expect to pay or receive support.

The Five Types of Spousal Support

Temporary support (pendente lite). Paid during the divorce proceedings to maintain the status quo while the case is pending. Temporary support ends when the final judgment is entered and is replaced by whatever the court orders as part of the decree. It is calculated quickly, often using guideline formulas, and is not a prediction of what the final award will be.

Rehabilitative support. The most common form in modern family law. Paid for a defined period to allow the lower-earning spouse to obtain education, training, or employment sufficient for self-support. A spouse who left the workforce for ten years to raise children might receive rehabilitative support for three to five years—enough time to complete a degree, obtain certification, or re-enter their profession. Courts expect the recipient to make genuine, documented efforts toward self-sufficiency. A spouse who collects rehabilitative support while making no effort to develop earning capacity invites modification or termination.

Permanent support. Increasingly rare and typically reserved for long marriages—twenty years or more—where the receiving spouse has limited earning potential due to age, health, or a decades-long absence from the workforce. Even "permanent" support is not always truly permanent: it terminates upon the recipient's remarriage, often terminates or is modifiable upon cohabitation with a new partner, and ends upon the death of either party.

Reimbursement support. Awarded when one spouse made specific financial sacrifices to support the other's education or career advancement—paying for medical school tuition, supporting the family while a spouse completed a law degree, or funding a business startup. Reimbursement compensates for that investment and is not based on ongoing need.

Lump-sum support. A single payment or a fixed series of payments totaling a defined amount. Lump-sum awards provide finality—no ongoing obligation, no future modification, no enforcement battles over monthly payments. They are useful when the paying spouse has liquidity and both parties prefer a clean break.

What Courts Evaluate

When the parties cannot agree on support, the court applies a multi-factor analysis. The specific statutory factors vary by state, but the recurring themes are:

- Duration of the marriage—the longer the marriage, the stronger the case for support and the longer the duration of the award

- Income disparity between the spouses—the wider the gap, the more likely support will be ordered

- Each spouse's earning capacity—not just current income, but what each person could earn given their education, skills, work history, and the local job market

- The standard of living established during the marriage—courts aim to prevent a dramatic post-divorce decline for the lower-earning spouse

- Age and health of each spouse—a fifty-eight-year-old with chronic health conditions faces different employment prospects than a thirty-four-year-old in good health

- Contributions to the marriage, including non-financial contributions—homemaking, child-rearing, supporting the other spouse's career, and managing the household are recognized as economic contributions even though they produce no paycheck

- The receiving spouse's efforts toward self-sufficiency—a spouse who has taken concrete steps to develop earning capacity (enrolling in school, completing job training, interviewing) strengthens their request

- Marital fault, in states that still consider it—adultery, abandonment, or cruelty may affect whether support is awarded, the amount, or the duration, depending on the jurisdiction

The Stay-at-Home Spouse

If you left the workforce to raise children, manage the household, or support your spouse's career, the law recognizes that your economic sacrifice created a dependency that the marriage was supposed to sustain. Your earning capacity today is not what it was when you left the workforce, and the gap between what you can earn now and what you would have earned had you continued working represents real economic damage.

Courts understand this. But they also expect you to demonstrate a willingness to re-enter the workforce, develop new skills, or pursue education that leads to self-support. The spouse who actively pursues rehabilitation—enrolling in classes, completing certifications, interviewing for positions—earns judicial sympathy. The spouse who makes no effort and relies on the argument that they "shouldn't have to work" earns judicial skepticism, particularly in shorter marriages.

WHAT I'VE SEEN: The Twenty-Year Gap

Claire left her teaching career when her first child was born. For twenty-one years, she managed the household, raised three children, volunteered at their schools, and supported her husband Alan's climb from associate to managing partner at an engineering firm. Alan earned $340,000 annually. Claire's last reported income, twenty-one years earlier, was $38,000. Her teaching certificate had lapsed. She had no recent work experience, no updated credentials, and no professional network. A vocational evaluator assessed Claire's earning capacity at $32,000 to $45,000—achievable within two to three years if she renewed her certification and re-entered the field. The court awarded rehabilitative support of $8,500 per month for five years, stepping down to $5,000 per month for an additional three years, with a review at year eight. Claire used the first two years to renew her teaching license, complete a master's degree in special education, and secure a position paying $54,000. The support structure gave her the runway she needed. Alan's obligation, while substantial, reflected the economic reality

110

that twenty-one years of Claire's unpaid labor had contributed directly to his ability to earn $340,000.

Imputed Income and Voluntary Underemployment

Just as courts impute income in child support cases, they do the same in alimony proceedings. A spouse who quits a job, declines promotions, retires early, or deliberately reduces hours to manipulate the support calculation faces judicial imputation—the court assigns an income based on what that person could reasonably earn.

This applies on both sides. A paying spouse who suddenly reports reduced income invites scrutiny. A receiving spouse who claims inability to work despite being young, healthy, and educated invites the same.

WHAT I'VE SEEN: The Convenient Career Change

Daniel, a pharmaceutical sales representative earning $195,000, resigned from his position three months before the alimony hearing and took a part-time job at a garden center paying $28,000. He told the court he had experienced "burnout" and needed to prioritize his mental health. His ex-wife's attorney subpoenaed Daniel's LinkedIn profile, which showed he had been actively networking with competitors and had told a former colleague in a message—produced during discovery—that he planned to 'lay low until the support order is set, then go back to real work.' The judge imputed income at $195,000, cited the LinkedIn message as evidence of deliberate manipulation, and awarded alimony based on Daniel's actual earning capacity. The garden center job did not reduce Daniel's obligation by a single dollar. It did, however, destroy his credibility on every other contested issue in the case.

Vocational Evaluations

When earning capacity is disputed, courts may order a vocational evaluation—an assessment by a certified professional who analyzes the spouse's education, work history, skills, physical and mental health, and the local labor market to determine what that person could reasonably earn. The evaluator interviews the spouse, reviews records, researches job openings, and produces a report estimating earning potential.

If you are the spouse claiming limited earning capacity, cooperate fully with the vocational evaluation. Refusal or obstruction suggests that you know your earning potential is higher than you are representing. If you are the spouse asserting that your partner can earn more than they claim, the vocational evaluation is your most powerful tool. Request one.

The Relationship Between Alimony and Property Division

Alimony and property division are not independent calculations. They are interconnected components of the same financial settlement. A spouse who receives a larger share of marital assets may receive less alimony—or none. A spouse who receives fewer assets may receive higher or longer support to compensate.

This interplay creates negotiation opportunities. A paying spouse who would rather make a larger one-time property transfer than pay monthly support for years may propose a lump-sum offset. A receiving spouse who values monthly income over illiquid assets (a house that requires maintenance, a retirement account that cannot be accessed for decades) may prefer higher support in exchange for fewer assets.

The key is understanding that the total financial package—assets plus support—determines the outcome, not either component in isolation. A settlement that gives you the house but provides no support may leave you asset-rich and cash-poor. A settlement with generous monthly support but no property leaves you vulnerable if the support is later modified or the paying spouse defaults.

> **Core Principle:** *Spousal support is neither charity nor punishment. It is a legally defined obligation based on specific, analyzable factors. Understanding those factors—and presenting evidence that addresses them directly—determines whether the number protects you or surprises you.*

CHAPTER 18

Negotiating, Settling, or Litigating Spousal Support

Most alimony outcomes are negotiated, not imposed. The number that appears in your final decree is far more likely to emerge from settlement discussions, mediation, or collaborative negotiation than from a judge's ruling after trial. Understanding how to position yourself in those negotiations—whether you expect to pay or receive—gives you influence over the result that passively waiting for a judicial decision does not.

Negotiation Strategy for the Receiving Spouse

Your leverage rests on three pillars: documented need, the paying spouse's demonstrated ability to pay, and a clear plan for what you will do with the support period. Courts respond to recipients who present a concrete rehabilitation plan—I will use rehabilitative support to complete this certification, re-enter this profession, and achieve self-sufficiency by this date—far more favorably than those who simply assert that they need money without articulating a path forward.

- Document your monthly expenses in granular detail. Not round numbers. Actual bills, receipts, and bank statements showing the cost of maintaining the household.

- Present a career rehabilitation timeline. If you need education or training, identify the program, the cost, the duration, and the projected salary upon completion.

- Demonstrate efforts already underway. Have you enrolled in classes? Updated your resume? Met with a career counselor? Evidence of initiative strengthens your request.

- Quantify the economic sacrifice. What would your career have looked like had you continued working? What was your trajectory before you left the workforce? Expert testimony or a vocational evaluation can establish this.

Negotiation Strategy for the Paying Spouse

Your goal is to limit the amount and duration of the obligation while protecting yourself against open-ended, indefinite payments. The most effective approach is not to argue that your spouse doesn't deserve support—which antagonizes the court—but to demonstrate that the obligation should be bounded, structured, and tied to specific milestones.

- Propose a step-down schedule: full support for the first two years, reduced by 25 percent in year three, reduced again in year five, terminating at a defined date.

- Include a cohabitation trigger: if the receiving spouse begins living with a new romantic partner, support is suspended or terminated. Many states recognize cohabitation as a basis for modification, but it must be addressed in the agreement.

- Negotiate a lump-sum buyout if you have the liquidity. A single payment eliminates the ongoing obligation, removes the risk of enforcement disputes, and provides certainty for both parties.

- Request a vocational evaluation if your spouse claims inability to work. Let an independent professional assess earning capacity rather than accepting self-reported limitations at face value.

- Address life insurance. If you are ordered to pay support, the court may require you to maintain a life insurance policy naming the receiving spouse as beneficiary to protect against the obligation terminating prematurely upon your death.

WHAT I'VE SEEN: The Buyout That Saved $127,000

Mitchell owed his ex-wife, Tara, $4,200 per month in rehabilitative alimony for seven years—a total obligation of $352,800. Mitchell's attorney proposed a lump-sum buyout of $225,000, funded by Mitchell's share of the proceeds from the sale of the marital home. Tara's attorney initially rejected the offer, arguing that monthly payments provided ongoing security. Mitchell's attorney presented a calculation: after accounting for the tax-neutral treatment of alimony under post-2018 law, the time value of money, and the risk that Mitchell could seek modification if his income changed, the present value of the seven-year stream was approximately $285,000. The $225,000 lump sum represented a modest discount for immediate certainty. Tara accepted. Mitchell saved approximately $127,000 in total payments. Tara received $225,000 in cash without the risk that Mitchell would lose his job, file for modification, or simply stop paying—forcing her to spend money she didn't have on enforcement. Both parties walked away with a clean financial break. Neither returned to court.

Tax Treatment After 2018

For divorce agreements executed after December 31, 2018, alimony is no longer deductible by the paying spouse and no longer taxable income to the receiving spouse. This is a significant shift from prior law, where the deduction incentivized higher support payments because the tax benefit reduced the net cost to the payer.

Under current law, the paying spouse bears the full economic burden of every dollar of support. This makes the gross amount more consequential and eliminates the tax-planning strategies that previously allowed both parties to benefit from the deduction/inclusion asymmetry.

If your divorce was finalized before January 1, 2019, and your agreement provides for deductible alimony, that treatment continues unless the agreement is modified. Be cautious about modifications that could inadvertently shift the tax treatment. Consult a tax professional before agreeing to any changes.

Protective Clauses Every Support Agreement Should Include

- A defined termination date—even for "permanent" support, include a review date or sunset provision

- Automatic termination upon remarriage of the receiving spouse

- A cohabitation clause defining what constitutes cohabitation (shared residence, shared expenses, holding out as a couple) and specifying whether it triggers termination, suspension, or review

- Step-down provisions reducing the monthly amount at defined intervals

- A self-sufficiency review clause requiring the receiving spouse to demonstrate ongoing efforts toward employment at specified intervals

- A life insurance requirement securing the obligation in the event of the paying spouse's death

- A disability provision addressing what happens if the paying spouse becomes unable to work

- An acceleration clause allowing the remaining obligation to be paid in a lump sum at the paying spouse's election

Core Principle: *The strongest alimony outcome is one you negotiate with clear eyes and complete financial information—not one imposed by a judge working with limited evidence and limited time. The negotiating table gives you options. The courtroom gives you a ruling.*

CHAPTER 19

Modifying and Terminating Spousal Support

Spousal support orders are not carved in stone. They are modifiable when circumstances change materially—and terminable when specific conditions are met. Whether you are paying more than your current situation justifies or receiving less than your changed needs require, the law provides a path to adjustment. But it requires action. Support orders do not modify themselves.

Grounds for Modification

A court will consider modifying a support order when there has been a substantial, material change in circumstances since the order was entered. The change must be significant and ongoing—not temporary, not speculative, and not self-created.

For the Paying Spouse

- Involuntary job loss, company closure, or industry-wide downturn
- Serious illness or disability that reduces earning capacity

- Retirement at a reasonable age (courts evaluate whether the timing is legitimate or designed to reduce income)
- Significant involuntary income reduction (pay cuts, loss of bonuses, business decline)

For the Receiving Spouse

- Increased need due to medical expenses, disability, or loss of employment
- A significant increase in the paying spouse's income that was not anticipated at the time of the original order
- Changed circumstances that make the original award inadequate to meet basic needs

The same warning that applies in child support applies here: if your income drops, file for modification immediately. Do not wait. Do not simply stop paying. Arrearages accumulate from the date of the existing order, not from the date you file. Every month of delay is a month of debt at the full original amount.

WHAT I'VE SEEN: The Retirement That Almost Worked

Howard, age sixty-two, retired from his corporate position and filed to terminate his $6,800 monthly alimony obligation, arguing that he no longer had income to pay. His ex-wife's attorney presented evidence that Howard had received a $1.2 million severance package, held $2.3 million in retirement accounts, and had begun collecting $4,100 per month in Social Security benefits. Howard's attorney argued that retirement at sixty-two was reasonable and that Howard should not be forced to continue working solely to fund alimony. The judge agreed that retirement at sixty-two was reasonable—but found that Howard's total financial resources, including investment income and Social Security, gave him the capacity to continue paying support at a reduced rate. The obligation was modified from $6,800 to $3,900 per month. Howard achieved a reduction but not *elimination. The court looked past the absence of a paycheck to the reality of his financial position.*

Automatic Termination Triggers

- Remarriage of the receiving spouse—in virtually every jurisdiction, this terminates the obligation automatically
- Death of either party (though some agreements provide for payments from the estate)
- Expiration of the defined term in the order
- Cohabitation with a new romantic partner, in jurisdictions that recognize it—though proving cohabitation often requires evidence of shared residence, shared finances, and holding out as a couple

The Cohabitation Battle

Cohabitation clauses are among the most heavily litigated provisions in support orders. The paying spouse alleges that the receiving spouse is living with a new partner and should no longer receive support. The receiving spouse denies cohabitation or argues that the relationship does not meet the legal definition.

What constitutes cohabitation varies by jurisdiction but generally requires more than occasional overnight visits. Courts look for shared residence, shared financial obligations (rent, utilities, groceries), presenting as a couple publicly, and the economic benefit the new partner provides to the receiving spouse. Evidence includes mail delivery records, utility accounts, vehicle registration, social media posts, neighbor testimony, and surveillance.

WHAT I'VE SEEN: The Boyfriend Who Didn't Officially Move In

Sharon's alimony agreement included a cohabitation clause providing for termination if she "resided with an unrelated adult in a conjugal relationship." Her ex-husband, Craig, hired a private investigator after learning that Sharon's boyfriend, Luke, appeared to be living at her home. The investigator documented Luke's vehicle in the driveway every night for forty-three consecutive days. Luke's mail was being delivered to Sharon's address. Luke's lease on his own apartment had expired and not been renewed. And Sharon had posted a photograph on Facebook captioned 'Home sweet home' showing her and Luke cooking dinner in her kitchen—three months after telling Craig that Luke 'stayed over occasionally.' Sharon's attorney argued that Luke maintained a separate mailing address (a P.O. box he had opened two weeks before the hearing), that he was merely a frequent guest, and that no formal cohabitation existed. The judge reviewed the surveillance records, the expired lease, the mail delivery evidence, and the social media post, and found cohabitation established. Alimony was terminated. Sharon's attempt to maintain the fiction of separate residences was dismantled by evidence that told a different story than her testimony.

When the Receiving Spouse Refuses to Pursue Self-Sufficiency

Rehabilitative support is designed with an expiration date in mind. The receiving spouse is expected to use the support period productively—developing skills, obtaining employment, building toward financial independence. When a receiving spouse makes no effort toward self-sufficiency—declining to pursue education, refusing to seek employment, or rejecting job opportunities below a subjective standard—the paying spouse has grounds to seek modification or termination.

Courts evaluate whether the receiving spouse's failure to rehabilitate is voluntary or involuntary. A spouse with documented health limitations or legitimate barriers to employment may retain support. A spouse who simply chose not to work faces imputation of earning capacity and potential reduction or termination of the award.

Strategic Considerations for Post-Judgment Alimony Disputes

- Keep meticulous records of your income, expenses, and any communications related to support

- Document the receiving spouse's lifestyle, employment status, and living arrangements if you believe modification is warranted

- File for modification promptly when circumstances change—do not accumulate arrears and hope for retroactive adjustment

- Understand that arrearages in spousal support, like child support, can be enforced through contempt, wage garnishment, and other collection mechanisms

- Negotiate modification terms before filing a motion when possible—agreed modifications are less expensive and less antagonistic than litigated ones

- Consult with a tax professional before agreeing to modification of pre-2019 alimony orders, as changes may affect the tax treatment

Core Principle: *Alimony does not have to last forever. Understanding when and how it can be modified protects both the payer and the recipient. The law provides mechanisms for adjustment. Using them requires awareness, documentation, and timely action.*

Property division is the most documentation-intensive phase of divorce. Every asset, every debt, every classification depends on records.

PART VI

PROPERTY DIVISION: PROTECTING WHAT YOU BUILT

Everything you own, everything you owe, and everything you built during this marriage is now on the table. The house, the retirement accounts, the business, the cars, the debt, the furniture, the cryptocurrency your spouse bought three years ago—all of it must be identified, classified, valued, and divided.

Property division is where the largest dollar amounts change hands in divorce. It is also where the most expensive mistakes are made—not through bad luck, but through ignorance. Clients who do not understand the difference between marital and separate property, who do not know what a QDRO is, who assume the house is always an asset rather than a liability, who fail to investigate whether their spouse is hiding money—these clients leave hundreds of thousands of dollars on the table. The five chapters ahead ensure you are not one of them.

CHAPTER 20

Property Division Fundamentals — Community Property vs. Equitable Distribution

The framework your state applies to property division determines everything. It dictates what is divisible, how it is divided, and what arguments carry weight before the court. Two systems dominate American family law, and they operate on fundamentally different premises.

The Two Frameworks

Community Property

Approximately nine states—Arizona, California, Idaho, Louisiana, Nevada, New Mexico, Texas, Washington, and Wisconsin—follow community property principles. The core rule: anything earned or acquired by either spouse during the marriage belongs equally to both, regardless of whose name is on the account, the title, or the paycheck. A surgeon who earns $600,000 per year and a stay-at-home parent who earns nothing both own half of that income. A house purchased during the marriage with marital funds is owned 50/50 even if only one spouse's name appears on the deed.

Community property starts with a presumption of equal division. Courts can deviate, but the baseline expectation is a 50/50 split of community assets and community debts. Separate property—assets owned before the marriage, gifts received individually, and inheritances—remains with the spouse who owns it, provided it has not been commingled with community funds.

Equitable Distribution

The remaining states follow equitable distribution. "Equitable" means fair—not equal. The court considers a range of factors and divides marital property in whatever proportion it determines to be just under the circumstances. A 50/50 split is common but not guaranteed, and deviations of 60/40 or even 70/30 occur when the factors support them.

Equitable distribution factors typically include the duration of the marriage, each spouse's income and earning capacity, age and health, contributions to the marriage (including homemaking), the economic circumstances of each spouse at the time of division, tax consequences, whether one spouse dissipated marital assets, and any other factor the court deems relevant to a fair outcome.

WHAT I'VE SEEN: The 60/40 Split Nobody Expected

Lena and Phillip divorced after fourteen years. Phillip assumed the division would be roughly equal—they lived in an equitable distribution state, and both had worked throughout the marriage. But Lena's attorney presented evidence that Phillip had dissipated approximately $95,000 in marital funds over three years—$42,000 spent on gifts, travel, and hotel rooms for an extramarital relationship, $28,000 in gambling losses he had concealed, and $25,000 in luxury purchases made after the separation without Lena's knowledge. The court classified the dissipated funds as Phillip's 'advance' on the marital estate and adjusted the division accordingly. Lena received 62 percent of the remaining assets. Phillip received 38 percent—plus the $95,000 he had already spent. The 'equitable' division *was technically equal once the dissipation was accounted for. But Phillip's share of the liquid assets available at divorce was dramatically smaller than he had anticipated.*

Marital Property vs. Separate Property

The classification question—is this asset marital or separate?—is the threshold issue in every property division case. Get the classification wrong, and you either forfeit assets you should have kept or fail to claim assets you were entitled to share.

Marital property: Assets acquired during the marriage through the labor, effort, or expenditure of either spouse. Wages, bonuses, commissions, business income, retirement contributions made during the marriage, real estate purchased with marital funds, and appreciation on marital assets are all marital property.

Separate property: Assets owned by one spouse before the marriage, gifts received by one spouse individually during the marriage, inheritances regardless of when received, and personal injury awards for pain and suffering (in most jurisdictions). Separate property retains its character only if it is kept separate.

Transmutation and Commingling: How Separate Property Becomes Marital

This is where fortunes are lost through carelessness. Separate property can lose its protected status and become marital property through two processes:

Commingling occurs when separate funds are mixed with marital funds in a way that makes them indistinguishable. If you deposit a $50,000 inheritance into the joint checking account that pays the mortgage, groceries, and credit card bills, that inheritance has been commingled with marital funds. Tracing it back to its separate origin becomes difficult—sometimes impossible—and courts may classify the entire account as marital.

Transmutation occurs when one spouse treats separate property as marital property through actions or intent. Adding your spouse's name to the title of a home you owned before the marriage. Using marital funds to pay the mortgage, taxes, and maintenance on a pre-marital property. Depositing your separate inheritance into a joint investment account titled in both names. Each of these actions can transmute separate property into marital property.

WHAT I'VE SEEN: The Inheritance That Vanished

Bridget received a $175,000 inheritance from her grandmother during the seventh year of her marriage. She deposited it into the couple's joint savings account with the intention of using it as a down payment on a larger home. Over the next four years, the couple drew from the account for vacations, home repairs, car purchases, and daily expenses. When Bridget filed for divorce, she claimed the $175,000 as separate property. Her husband's attorney asked a single question: 'Can you identify which dollars in the joint account are the inheritance and which are marital earnings?' Bridget could not. The money had been commingled beyond recognition. The court classified the entire account as marital. Bridget lost $87,500—half of her grandmother's gift—because she failed to keep it in a separate account bearing only her name. Had she deposited the inheritance into an individual account and never mixed it with marital funds, it would have remained hers entirely.

The Date of Valuation

When are assets valued for purposes of division? The answer varies by state and can swing the outcome by tens or hundreds of thousands of dollars. Some states value assets as of the date of separation. Others use the date the divorce complaint was filed. Still others use the date of trial or the date of the final decree.

The difference matters most for volatile assets—stock portfolios, real estate in appreciating or declining markets, business interests, and cryptocurrency. A retirement account worth $400,000 on the date of separation may be worth $340,000 or $480,000 by the time trial occurs. The valuation date determines which number the court uses.

Know your state's rule and plan accordingly. If your assets are appreciating and the valuation date is the date of trial, delay may benefit you. If they are declining, delay works against you. This is a conversation your attorney should have with you early in the case.

Why "Equitable" Rarely Means "Equal"

In equitable distribution states, judges weigh multiple factors that can justify unequal division:

- A long marriage with significant income disparity favors a larger share to the lower-earning spouse

- A spouse who dissipated marital assets through gambling, affairs, addiction, or reckless spending may receive a reduced share

- A spouse whose separate property was used to benefit the marriage (paying down the mortgage with premarital savings, for example) may receive credit

- Health or disability that limits one spouse's ability to earn income after the divorce

- A spouse who sacrificed career advancement to support the other spouse's professional development

- Tax consequences that make the nominal value of assets misleading—a $200,000 401(k) is worth less than $200,000 in a bank account because the retirement funds will be taxed upon withdrawal

Core Principle: *What you do not know about your own finances can cost you everything in divorce. Financial ignorance is the most expensive mistake clients make. Before you negotiate a single dollar, understand what you own, what you owe, what is marital, and what is separate.*

CHAPTER 21

The Marital Home, Real Estate, and Major Assets

The family home is the most emotionally charged asset in divorce. It is where the children grew up, where holidays happened, where the marriage existed in physical form. Clients fight for the house with an intensity that has nothing to do with its appraised value—and that intensity produces some of the most financially destructive decisions I have witnessed in nearly forty years of practice.

The Three Options for the Family Home

Option 1: Sell the House and Split the Proceeds

The cleanest outcome. The house is listed, sold at fair market value, the mortgage and closing costs are paid from the proceeds, and the remaining equity is divided. Both parties walk away with liquid assets and no ongoing financial entanglement with their former spouse. For most families, this is the most rational choice—and the one most frequently resisted for emotional reasons.

133

Option 2: One Spouse Buys Out the Other

One spouse keeps the house and compensates the other for their share of the equity, either through a cash payment, an offset against other marital assets (receiving less of the retirement accounts, for example), or a promissory note. The buying spouse must refinance the mortgage in their name alone—removing the other spouse from the loan—within a specified period, typically six to twelve months.

This option works only if the buying spouse qualifies for refinancing on their single income. If they cannot qualify, both names remain on the mortgage, and the selling spouse retains liability for a property they no longer own or occupy—a dangerous position.

Option 3: Deferred Sale (Co-Ownership)

In some cases, particularly when young children are involved, courts allow the custodial parent to remain in the home until a triggering event—the youngest child reaching eighteen, the custodial parent remarrying, or a defined number of years—at which point the home is sold and proceeds divided. During the interim, both parties may share responsibility for the mortgage, taxes, and maintenance.

Deferred sale preserves stability for the children but creates ongoing financial interdependence between two people who are trying to separate their lives. If the relationship between the parties is high-conflict, deferred sale often generates more disputes than it prevents.

WHAT I'VE SEEN: The House She Couldn't Afford to Keep

Rachel insisted on keeping the family home—a four-bedroom house with a $2,400 monthly mortgage, $6,800 annual property taxes, and ongoing maintenance costs that had averaged $8,000 per year during the marriage. Rachel's post-divorce income, including alimony, was $5,200 per month. Her attorney warned her that the numbers did not work. Rachel's therapist told her the house represented stability *for the children. Rachel chose the house over a larger share of the retirement accounts and a cash settlement that would have provided a financial cushion. Within eighteen months, Rachel was behind on the mortgage, had deferred $14,000 in necessary repairs, and was carrying $11,000 in credit card debt accumulated to cover household expenses. She listed the house in a declining market and sold it for $40,000 less than its appraised value at the time of the divorce. The retirement accounts she had traded away were worth $210,000— liquid, growing, and inflation-protected. The house she kept cost her $40,000 in lost value, $14,000 in deferred maintenance, $11,000 in debt, and the financial security the retirement funds would have provided. One emotionally driven decision. A quarter of a million dollars in damage.*

Appraisals and Valuation Disputes

Before the house can be divided, it must be valued. Each spouse typically retains an independent appraiser. If the appraisals differ significantly—and they often do—the court may order a third appraisal, average the competing valuations, or make its own determination based on the evidence.

Appraisers are not neutral in the way people assume. The appraiser hired by the spouse who wants to buy the house has an incentive to produce a lower valuation, reducing the buyout cost. The appraiser hired by the spouse who wants to sell or receive their share has an incentive to produce a higher valuation. Understanding this dynamic helps you evaluate the numbers you receive.

Investment Properties and Rental Income

Rental properties require careful analysis beyond their appraised value. The relevant figure is not what the property would sell for—it is the net economic value after accounting for the mortgage balance, deferred maintenance, rental income, management costs, and tax consequences of sale (including capital gains and depreciation recapture). A rental property appraised at $350,000 with a $280,000 mortgage, $30,000 in deferred repairs, and $45,000 in potential depreciation recapture taxes is worth far less than its headline number suggests.

Vehicles, Personal Property, and the Small Disputes That Consume Big Resources

Furniture, jewelry, art, electronics, vehicles, tools, and household contents must also be addressed. These disputes should be resolved quickly and with minimal cost. A fight over a $3,000 dining room set that generates $2,000 in attorney fees is a net loss for both parties.

The practical approach: each party makes a list of the personal property items they want. Items that appear on only one list go to that person. Items that appear on both lists are negotiated, alternating selections, or valued and offset against other assets. Do not litigate the silverware.

> **Core Principle:** *Do not let emotion drive real estate decisions. Run the numbers. A house you cannot afford is not a victory—it is a trap disguised as stability.*

CHAPTER 22

Retirement Accounts, Pensions, and Financial Instruments

In my experience, the retirement account is the single most under-valued asset in divorce. Clients fixate on the house—the asset they can see and touch—while the 401(k), the pension, or the stock option package sits quietly in the background holding more money than the equity in the home. Failing to divide retirement assets correctly is not a minor error. It is the most financially devastating mistake in the entire process.

What Is Divisible

The marital portion of a retirement account is the value that accrued during the marriage. If your spouse opened a 401(k) five years before you married and has contributed for twenty years total, the marital portion covers the fifteen years of marriage—not the full twenty. Contributions made before the marriage, and the growth attributable to those premarital contributions, remain the account holder's separate property.

The same principle applies to pensions, IRAs, 403(b) accounts, deferred compensation plans, and stock option grants. The marital portion is determined by the overlap between the marriage and the accumulation period.

The QDRO: The Order You Cannot Skip

A Qualified Domestic Relations Order—a QDRO, pronounced "quadro"—is a specialized court order that directs a retirement plan administrator to divide the account between the spouses. Without a QDRO, the non-employee spouse has no legal claim to the retirement funds, regardless of what the divorce decree says.

This point cannot be overstated: the divorce decree alone does not divide a retirement account. The decree says the account should be divided. The QDRO tells the plan administrator how to divide it. Without the QDRO, the plan administrator will not release a single dollar to the non-employee spouse.

WHAT I'VE SEEN: The QDRO That Was Never Filed

Adrienne's divorce decree awarded her 50 percent of her ex-husband Paul's 401(k), valued at $310,000 at the time of the decree—her share was $155,000. Adrienne's attorney told her a QDRO would be prepared and filed. The attorney did not follow through. Adrienne assumed it had been handled. Three years later, when Adrienne needed the funds for a down payment on a house, she contacted the plan administrator and was told no QDRO had ever been received. Paul's account had grown to $385,000 in the interim, but Adrienne's share was still based on the original $310,000 valuation because the decree specified a dollar amount rather than a percentage. Adrienne hired a new attorney to prepare and file the QDRO—at a cost of $3,500. She received her $155,000, but had the QDRO been filed promptly and specified a percentage rather than a fixed amount, she would have received $192,500. The three-year delay and the drafting error cost Adrienne $37,500. A QDRO that should have been filed within thirty days of the decree sat in a *drawer for three years. That drawer was the most expensive piece of furniture in the divorce.*

Pensions and Defined Benefit Plans

Pensions are more complex than 401(k) accounts because they pay a monthly benefit at retirement rather than holding a lump-sum balance. Dividing a pension requires determining the marital portion—typically calculated using the coverture fraction, which is the number of years of credited service during the marriage divided by the total years of service at retirement.

If your spouse has a pension through a government employer, a union, or a long-tenure corporate position, that pension may be the single largest asset in the marriage—worth more than the house, the savings accounts, and the vehicles combined. Do not accept a quick settlement without understanding the pension's present value.

Stock Options, RSUs, and Deferred Compensation

Vested options and RSUs can be exercised now and have a quantifiable present value. The marital portion of vested options is typically divisible.

Unvested options and RSUs cannot be exercised until a future vesting date. Courts split on how to handle them. Some divide them now using a present-value calculation. Others apply an "if, as, and when" approach—the non-employee spouse receives their share only when and if the options vest.

Deferred compensation plans pay out at a future date, often upon retirement or termination. The marital portion accumulated during the marriage is divisible, but the timing and tax treatment of the payout add complexity.

If your spouse works in technology, finance, medicine, or any field where equity compensation is a significant portion of total pay, these instruments may represent hundreds of thousands of dollars in marital value. Do not ignore them because they are difficult to understand.

Social Security Benefits After Divorce

If your marriage lasted ten years or longer, you may be eligible to receive Social Security benefits based on your ex-spouse's earnings record—even if your ex-spouse has remarried. This benefit does not reduce your ex-spouse's benefit. It is a separate entitlement.

To qualify, you must have been married for at least ten years, be currently unmarried (or, if remarried, the subsequent marriage ended), be at least sixty-two years old, and your own Social Security benefit must be less than what you would receive on your ex-spouse's record. If you are approaching the ten-year mark and considering divorce, the timing of your filing may have significant financial consequences.

Cryptocurrency and Digital Assets

Bitcoin, Ethereum, and other digital currencies present unique challenges. They can be held in wallets that are difficult to trace, transferred across borders instantly, and valued at wildly different amounts depending on the day. A spouse holding cryptocurrency may not disclose it voluntarily, and traditional discovery tools may not capture it without specific, targeted requests.

If you suspect your spouse holds cryptocurrency, request discovery specifically targeting digital wallets, exchange accounts (Coinbase, Kraken, Binance), blockchain transactions, and any hardware wallets. Forensic specialists in digital asset tracing can follow the blockchain to identify holdings that traditional financial discovery would miss.

> **Core Principle:** *Retirement assets represent real, substantial money. Failing to divide them correctly through proper QDRO procedures is the most financially devastating error in divorce. Do not trade your future for the illusion of present-day victory.*

CHAPTER 23

Business Ownership, Professional Practices, and Complex Assets

When a business is part of the marital estate, the divorce becomes a financial investigation. The value of a closely held company, a medical practice, a law firm partnership, or a franchise operation is not printed on a statement. It must be determined through expert analysis—and every dollar of that valuation affects what each spouse receives.

Business owners facing divorce often believe they can control the narrative. They know the books. They sign the checks. They decide what the tax return shows. What they frequently do not appreciate is that family courts and forensic accountants have seen every technique, every shelter, and every creative accounting strategy. The spouse who assumes their financial picture cannot be reconstructed is almost always wrong.

The Three Standard Valuation Approaches

Income Approach

Values the business based on its ability to generate future income. A forensic accountant analyzes historical earnings, normalizes them to remove one-time expenses and owner perks, and applies a capitalization rate or discount to project the present value of the income stream. This method is most common for service businesses and professional practices where cash flow is the primary value driver.

Market Approach

Compares the business to similar businesses that have recently been sold. Just as a house is appraised by comparing it to comparable sales, a business can be valued by examining transactions involving similar companies in the same industry and geographic area. This method works best when reliable comparable data exists—which is more common for franchises and standard business models than for unique or specialized operations.

Asset-Based Approach

Values the business based on the net value of its tangible and intangible assets minus its liabilities. This method is used most often for holding companies, real estate entities, and businesses being liquidated rather than sold as going concerns.

In practice, a forensic accountant may use more than one method and reconcile the results. The valuation is only as reliable as the data underlying it—which is why complete, honest financial disclosure is not optional.

Professional Practices and the Goodwill Problem

If your spouse is a doctor, dentist, attorney, CPA, or other professional, the practice has value beyond its physical assets. That additional value is called goodwill—the premium a buyer would pay for the practice's reputation, patient or client relationships, referral networks, and revenue stream.

Courts distinguish between two types of goodwill:

Enterprise goodwill is the value that would transfer to a buyer—the practice's location, staff, systems, equipment, brand recognition, and patient base. Enterprise goodwill is typically divisible as a marital asset.

Personal goodwill is the value attributable solely to the individual practitioner's personal skill, reputation, and relationships. Many states exclude personal goodwill from the marital estate on the theory that it cannot be sold or transferred—it walks out the door when the professional does.

The distinction matters enormously. A dental practice valued at $800,000 total might have $500,000 in enterprise goodwill (divisible) and $300,000 in personal goodwill (not divisible in many states). The classification can swing the property division by six figures.

WHAT I'VE SEEN: The Practice Worth Twice What He Claimed

Dr. Garrett owned a dermatology practice that he valued at $375,000 based on his own accountant's assessment. His wife's attorney retained an independent forensic valuator who analyzed five years of tax returns, accounts receivable, patient revenue trends, insurance reimbursement rates, and comparable practice sales. The independent valuation came in at $740,000. The discrepancy came from three sources: Dr. Garrett's accountant had used an artificially low earnings multiplier, had excluded $85,000 in annual personal expenses routed through the practice (a leased vehicle, country club membership, travel to conferences in resort destinations, and meals), and had undervalued the patient base by ignoring the practice's 94 percent retention rate—one of the highest in the region. The court adopted the independent valuation. Dr. Garrett's wife received credit for her marital share based on $740,000, not $375,000. The difference: approximately $182,500 in additional marital property *attributed to the practice. Dr. Garrett's attempt to undervalue the practice—using his own accountant rather than submitting to independent analysis—cost him precisely the amount he had tried to hide.*

Hidden Income in Cash-Intensive Businesses

Restaurants, construction companies, landscaping firms, car washes, salons, and any business that handles significant amounts of cash present a particular challenge. Revenue that passes through in currency without being deposited or reported can be extremely difficult to trace using traditional financial analysis.

Forensic accountants address this through bank deposit analysis (comparing total deposits to reported revenue to identify gaps), lifestyle analysis (comparing reported income to actual spending patterns), source-and-use-of-funds analysis (reconstructing where money came from and where it went), and cross-referencing vendor payments, supply purchases, and operating costs against reported revenue to identify mathematical impossibilities—a restaurant that purchases $200,000 in food and supplies but reports only $280,000 in revenue has margins that defy industry norms.

When to Hire a Forensic Accountant

Not every case requires forensic analysis. If your spouse is a salaried employee with a W-2, a 401(k), and no outside business interests, the financial picture is relatively transparent. But if any of the following red flags are present, forensic engagement is not optional:

- Your spouse owns or has an interest in a closely held business
- Reported income appears inconsistent with the family's lifestyle

- Your spouse's business is cash-intensive

- Your spouse has recently formed new business entities, LLCs, or trusts

- Financial documents are incomplete, inconsistent, or suspiciously difficult to obtain

- Your spouse controls the family finances and you have limited visibility into accounts

- There are transfers to family members, friends, or entities you do not recognize

- Your spouse's reported income has dropped significantly since the divorce was filed

Core Principle: *If your spouse owns a business, every dollar you fail to investigate is a dollar you may forfeit. Forensic diligence is not a luxury. It is the minimum required to protect your share of the marital estate.*

CHAPTER 24

Hidden Assets, Financial Fraud, and Dissipation

People hide money in divorce. Not all people. Not most people. But enough that every experienced family law attorney has seen it, pursued it, and watched the consequences fall on the spouse who thought they were clever enough to get away with it.

Concealment takes many forms—some sophisticated, some remarkably crude. The common thread is an assumption that the other spouse, the other attorney, or the court will not look hard enough to find what has been hidden. That assumption is frequently wrong.

Warning Signs of Concealed Assets

- Sudden claims of reduced income despite no visible change in lifestyle

- New accounts, LLCs, or entities created during or shortly before the divorce

- Large cash withdrawals with vague or inconsistent explanations

- Overpayments to the IRS (requesting a refund after the divorce is finalized)

- Loans to friends or family members that appeared for the first time during the proceedings

- Deferral of bonuses, commissions, or contracts until after the anticipated resolution date

- Purchase of expensive items (art, jewelry, collectibles) that are easily concealed and difficult to trace

- Cryptocurrency purchases or transfers to digital wallets

- An unusually cooperative attitude about property division combined with resistance to producing financial documents

Financial Discovery Tools

The legal system provides powerful tools to investigate financial concealment. Your attorney can deploy:

Interrogatories: Written questions under oath requiring detailed disclosure of assets, accounts, income sources, and financial transactions.

Document requests: Demands for production of bank statements, tax returns, business records, loan applications, credit card statements, brokerage account records, and any other financial documentation.

Subpoenas to third parties: Court orders directing banks, brokerage firms, employers, business partners, and other institutions to produce records directly—bypassing your spouse's control over what is disclosed.

Depositions: Sworn testimony where your spouse is questioned under oath about financial matters, with a court reporter recording every answer.

A spouse who lies in response to any of these tools commits perjury—a crime that courts take seriously in the context of divorce proceedings. False financial declarations, concealed accounts, and dishonest deposition testimony can result in sanctions, adverse inference (the court assumes the worst about what was hidden), disproportionate property division, contempt, and in extreme cases, criminal referral.

✦ ✦ ✦

Dissipation: Wasting What Belongs to Both of You

Dissipation is the legal term for one spouse wasting marital assets for a purpose unrelated to the marriage at a time when the marriage is breaking down. It is not the same as ordinary spending during the marriage. It is spending—or destruction of value—that occurs after the parties have separated, after a divorce has been filed, or during a period when one spouse was clearly acting to harm the other's financial interests.

Common forms of dissipation include:

- Gifts to an affair partner—jewelry, trips, rent payments, cash

- Gambling losses during the separation period

- Reckless or extravagant spending that depletes marital accounts

- Intentional destruction of marital property (damaging the house, wrecking a vehicle)

- Transferring assets to family members or friends with the intent to place them beyond the reach of the court

- Running up credit card debt on discretionary purchases after the separation

---

WHAT I'VE SEEN: The Girlfriend's Apartment

During the eighteen months between separation and trial, Gerald spent $78,000 in marital funds on his girlfriend: $32,000 in rent for an apartment he leased in her name, $18,000 on jewelry, $14,000 on vacations, and $14,000 on restaurant bills charged to a credit card linked to the marital bank account. Gerald's wife's attorney traced every expenditure through credit card statements, bank transfers, and receipts obtained during discovery. At trial, the judge classified the $78,000 as dissipation and credited it entirely to Gerald's side of the property division. In practical terms, Gerald's share of the remaining marital estate was reduced by $78,000—meaning his wife received that amount from other assets. Gerald had already spent the money. He now owed its equivalent from what was left. The girlfriend's apartment, the jewelry, and the vacations had been funded with money that belonged to both spouses. The court treated Gerald as though he had already received his share—$78,000 worth of it—and divided the remainder accordingly.

Offshore Accounts, Cryptocurrency, and Digital Concealment

Sophisticated concealment strategies present real challenges—but they are not impenetrable. Offshore accounts in jurisdictions with banking secrecy laws can sometimes be identified through FBAR filings (Report of Foreign Bank and Financial Accounts) that are required on federal tax returns. Cryptocurrency transactions are recorded on public blockchains and can be traced by forensic specialists. Digital payment platforms—Venmo, Zelle, Cash App, PayPal—create records that subpoenas can access.

The spouse who believes digital assets are invisible is operating on outdated assumptions. The tools available to forensic investigators have advanced as rapidly as the tools available to concealers.

Protective Measures You Can Take Now

- Document the family's financial position before filing: photograph or copy bank statements, tax returns, brokerage statements, retirement account records, business records, and insurance policies

- Note account numbers and balances for every financial account you are aware of

- Save copies of your spouse's pay stubs, bonus records, and employment agreements

- Photograph valuable personal property (art, jewelry, collections, vehicles) and note approximate values

- Monitor joint credit reports for new accounts, credit inquiries, or address changes you did not authorize

- Request copies of the last three to five years of joint tax returns from the IRS if you do not already have them

- Consult your attorney immediately if you notice unexplained withdrawals, new accounts, or transfers to unfamiliar entities

These steps are not adversarial. They are self-protective. You are not accusing your spouse of anything. You are ensuring that if concealment has occurred, you have a baseline from which the forensic trail can begin.

Core Principle: *Trust but verify. In divorce, complete financial transparency is mandatory, not aspirational. Courts punish concealment with sanctions, adverse inferences, and disproportionate division. The spouse who hides money almost always pays more than they would have paid by disclosing it honestly.*

Safety is the foundation. Documentation transforms lived experience into evidence the court can act on.

PART VII

DOMESTIC VIOLENCE, SUBSTANCE ABUSE, AND PROTECTIVE ORDERS

The five chapters ahead address the cases where safety, addiction, mental health, or psychological manipulation dominate the landscape. These are not rare circumstances. In my practice, some combination of domestic violence, substance abuse, or serious mental health instability surfaces in more than half of contested divorces. When any of these issues is present, the legal strategy, the evidentiary requirements, and the emotional stakes change completely.

If you are in danger, read Chapter 25 first. If your spouse is struggling with addiction, Chapter 27 applies whether you are the accusing party or the one being accused. If alienation is tearing your child away from you, Chapter 29 offers the framework for fighting back without destroying your credibility in the process.

Domestic Violence in Divorce — Safety, Evidence, and Legal Protection

If you are reading this chapter because you are in danger, your safety comes first. Before legal strategy, before evidence collection, before anything else—get safe. The National Domestic Violence Hotline is available 24 hours a day at 1-800-799-7233 (SAFE). They can help you develop a safety plan, locate shelter, and connect you with local resources. If you are in immediate danger, call 911.

What follows assumes you have secured your physical safety or are planning to do so. This chapter addresses how domestic violence intersects with every dimension of your divorce case and how to build the evidentiary record that protects you and your children in court.

Domestic Violence Beyond Physical Assault

Courts and legislatures have expanded the definition of domestic violence well beyond hitting, slapping, and shoving. Modern domestic violence law increasingly recognizes:

- Emotional and psychological abuse: persistent degradation, humiliation, threats, isolation from friends and family, and destruction of self-worth

- Coercive control: a sustained pattern of domination through monitoring, restricting movement, controlling finances, dictating daily decisions, and enforcing compliance through fear

- Financial abuse: withholding access to money, running up debt in the victim's name, destroying credit, controlling all financial information, and using economic dependence as a weapon

- Sexual abuse within the marriage: coerced sexual activity, refusal to honor boundaries, and assault disguised as marital entitlement

- Digital abuse: monitoring texts and emails, tracking location through phones or devices, installing spyware, impersonating the victim online, and distributing intimate images without consent

- Threats to harm children, pets, or property as instruments of control

Coercive control—the pattern of domination that may never involve a single act of physical violence—is increasingly recognized by courts as a form of domestic abuse that directly affects custody determinations. A spouse who controls every aspect of the household through fear, surveillance, and psychological manipulation may never leave a bruise, but the harm to the victim and the children is well documented in the clinical literature and is gaining traction in family courtrooms.

Building the Evidentiary Record

Domestic violence cases are won or lost on documentation. Your testimony alone, no matter how truthful, faces the challenge of competing with a composed abuser who denies everything—often with practiced sincerity. The evidence that tips the balance includes:

- Medical records documenting injuries, even if you did not disclose the true cause at the time—the records establish the physical harm; the explanation can be corrected later

- Police reports, even if no arrest was made—the report creates a contemporaneous record that the incident occurred

- Photographs of injuries, property damage, or threatening messages—timestamped and stored securely

- Text messages, voicemails, and emails containing threats, admissions, or abusive language

- Witness statements from anyone who observed the abuse or its aftermath—neighbors, friends, family members, coworkers who saw injuries

- Incident logs maintained contemporaneously: date, time, what happened, who witnessed it, and how it affected you and the children

- Records from domestic violence counselors, therapists, or shelter staff

- School records, pediatrician notes, or therapist records reflecting the impact on children

---

WHAT I'VE SEEN: The Pattern Nobody Believed Until They Saw It

---

For seven years, Deborah told her sister, her therapist, and eventually her attorney that her husband, Stuart, had never hit her—but that she lived in constant fear. Stuart controlled every dollar. He monitored her phone. He timed her grocery trips and questioned discrepancies. He told her daily that she was 'lucky anyone put up with her.' When she tried to enroll in a community college course, he canceled the registration from her account. When she spoke to a male neighbor, Stuart demanded she explain the conversation and then forbade her from walking outside alone. Stuart had never been arrested. There was no police report. No photograph of a bruise. The custody evaluator initially viewed Stuart as the more stable parent—he was calm, employed, and controlled. Deborah appeared anxious and uncertain. Then Deborah's attorney introduced four years of text messages. Over 6,000 messages documented Stuart's monitoring, his demands for real-time location photos, his financial restrictions, and his escalating threats when Deborah failed to comply. The therapist testified to the clinical pattern of coercive control. The evaluator reversed the initial assessment. The court found domestic violence based on the sustained pattern of psychological domination and awarded Deborah primary custody with Stuart's contact supervised. No bruise. No police report. Four years of text messages and a therapist who understood the pattern.

How Domestic Violence Affects Custody, Support, and Property

A finding of domestic violence reshapes the entire case:

- Custody: most states create a rebuttable presumption against awarding custody to the abusive parent. The abuser must demonstrate rehabilitation, completion of treatment, and that custody would serve the child's best interests despite the history of violence.

- Visitation: may be restricted to supervised contact, limited duration, or conditioned on completion of batterer intervention programs

- Spousal support: a finding of domestic violence may increase the amount or duration of support to the victim. In some jurisdictions, a perpetrator may be barred from receiving support entirely.

- Property division: courts may award a disproportionate share of marital property to the victim as a remedial measure

When the Abuser Weaponizes the Legal System

Abusers who are sophisticated enough to manipulate in private are often sophisticated enough to manipulate in court. Legal abuse—the use of the court system as a continuation of control—includes filing frivolous motions to drain the victim's financial resources, making false counter-allegations of abuse to muddy the record, seeking protective orders against the victim to create a narrative of mutual conflict, demanding excessive discovery to overwhelm and exhaust, and using every procedural tool available not to achieve a legal objective but to perpetuate the dynamic of domination.

If you are experiencing legal abuse, document the pattern. Track every filing, every motion, every hearing. A record showing twenty emergency motions in twelve months—none of which resulted in relief—tells a story that judges eventually recognize.

Core Principle: *Your safety is the non-negotiable foundation. Every other legal strategy builds on it. If you are in danger, get safe first. Then build the record.*

CHAPTER 26

Restraining Orders, Protective Orders, and Injunctions

Protective orders are among the most powerful tools in family law. They can remove an abuser from the home, establish temporary custody, prohibit contact, restrict firearms possession, and create criminal liability for violations—all on an emergency basis, sometimes within hours of filing. They can also be misused. A protective order filed for tactical advantage rather than genuine safety is identifiable, and courts respond to misuse with skepticism that taints the filer's credibility for the remainder of the case.

Types of Protective Orders

Emergency protective orders (EPOs) can be issued by law enforcement at the scene of a domestic violence incident, without a court hearing. They are temporary—typically lasting five to seven days—and are designed to provide immediate protection until the victim can seek a longer-term order from the court.

Temporary restraining orders (TROs) are issued by a judge based on the petitioner's sworn application, often without the respondent present (ex parte). They remain in effect until a full hearing, usually scheduled within fourteen to twenty-one days.

Permanent protective orders are issued after a full evidentiary hearing where both parties present testimony and evidence. "Permanent" is misleading—these orders typically last one to five years, with the option to renew. They carry the full weight of a court order, and violation is a criminal offense.

How to Obtain a Protective Order

The process begins with a sworn petition describing the abuse, the threat, and the relief you are requesting. Include specific incidents with dates, descriptions, and any evidence you can attach—photographs, police reports, medical records, threatening messages. The more specific and documented your petition, the more likely the court is to grant emergency relief.

At the ex parte stage, the standard is typically whether you have demonstrated an immediate threat of harm. At the full hearing, you must present evidence that domestic violence occurred and that continued protection is necessary. Your testimony matters, but corroborating evidence—police reports, medical records, photographs, witness testimony, text messages—strengthens your case.

What Protective Orders Accomplish

- No-contact provisions: the respondent is prohibited from contacting the petitioner directly or through third parties
- Exclusion from the residence: the respondent must leave the shared home, even if their name is on the lease or deed
- Temporary custody: the court may award temporary custody of children to the petitioner

- Stay-away provisions: the respondent must maintain a specified distance from the petitioner's home, workplace, and children's school

- Firearms restrictions: in most jurisdictions, an active protective order prohibits the respondent from possessing firearms—a federal prohibition under the Lautenberg Amendment

- Financial provisions: temporary support, exclusive use of a vehicle, and orders prohibiting the respondent from interfering with the petitioner's finances

Defending Against False or Exaggerated Claims

Protective orders are sometimes filed not because genuine danger exists but to gain tactical advantage in custody or property disputes—securing exclusive possession of the home, establishing temporary custody, or creating a record that damages the respondent's position.

If you have been served with a protective order you believe is false or exaggerated:

- Take the order seriously regardless of your belief about its validity. Comply with every provision. A violation—even of an order you believe is unjust—is a criminal offense.

- Retain an attorney immediately. The full hearing is your opportunity to present your side, and it will arrive quickly.

- Gather evidence that contradicts the allegations: text messages showing amicable communication, evidence of the petitioner's motive for tactical filing, witness testimony, and any documentation that undermines the claimed timeline.

- Do not contact the petitioner, directly or indirectly, to discuss the order. Even well-intentioned communication is a violation.

WHAT I'VE SEEN: The Order That Backfired

Renee filed for a protective order against her husband, Victor, two days before a scheduled custody mediation. Her petition alleged that Victor had 'threatened' her during a phone call. Victor's attorney subpoenaed the phone records and obtained Victor's recording of the conversation—legal in their one-party consent state. The recording captured a calm discussion about the parenting schedule. No threats. No raised voices. No language that any reasonable person would characterize as threatening. At the full hearing, the judge denied the permanent order and noted in the record that the petition 'appears to have been filed for the purpose of gaining tactical advantage in the pending custody dispute rather than in response to genuine fear.' That finding followed Renee through the rest of her case. When she raised legitimate concerns about Victor's behavior six months later, the judge weighed them against the earlier finding and discounted her credibility accordingly. The protective order she filed to gain an edge cost her the very thing she needed most: the court's trust.

Financial Injunctions and Asset Preservation Orders

Separate from domestic violence protective orders, many jurisdictions issue automatic temporary restraining orders (ATROs) at the time a divorce is filed. These prohibit both parties from dissipating marital assets, canceling insurance, hiding money, or destroying property. Violations are enforceable through contempt.

If your state does not have automatic ATROs, your attorney can request a financial injunction to prevent your spouse from depleting accounts, transferring property, or incurring new debt. Request this early—before the assets are moved, not after.

> **Core Principle:** *Protective orders are serious judicial instruments. Seek them when genuine danger exists. Misusing them for tactical advantage damages your credibility, and courts identify and punish the abuse.*

CHAPTER 27

Substance Abuse in Divorce — Both Sides of the Issue

This chapter speaks to two audiences. If your spouse has a substance abuse problem that is affecting your children or your safety, you need to know how to document it, prove it, and present it in a way that courts take seriously. If you are the person managing a substance use issue—whether active or in recovery—you need to understand how courts evaluate your situation and what you can do to protect your custody position and your credibility.

Both sides of this equation deserve honest guidance. What follows provides it.

How Courts Assess Substance Abuse

Courts do not treat all substance use identically. A glass of wine at dinner is not the same as driving with children in the car after four cocktails. A prescription for Adderall taken as directed is not the same as escalating opioid misuse that produces impaired parenting. Courts evaluate substance use along a spectrum:

- Recreational or social use that does not impair parenting—generally not a custody concern

- Problematic use that creates safety risks during parenting time—a legitimate concern requiring documentation

- Dependence or addiction that produces patterns of impaired judgment, neglect, erratic behavior, or dangerous environments for children—a serious factor in custody and credibility

The question the court asks is not "Does this person drink?" or "Does this person use substances?" The question is "Does this person's substance use impair their ability to provide safe, consistent, adequate parenting?"

Documenting Substance Abuse Credibly

Allegations without evidence are dismissed. Emotional accusations without specifics are counterproductive. What courts require:

- Specific incidents: dates, times, what you observed or what the children reported, in factual language

- Corroborating evidence: photographs of intoxication or impaired behavior, text messages admitting use, police reports for DUIs or related incidents, empty bottles or paraphernalia documented photographically

- Third-party observations: teachers, pediatricians, therapists, or other professionals who have noted signs of substance-related impairment in the parent or distress in the children

- Patterns over time: courts respond to documented patterns far more powerfully than to a single isolated incident

---

WHAT I'VE SEEN: The DUI That Changed Everything

For two years, Allison told her attorney that her ex-husband Brian was drinking during his parenting weekends. Brian denied it. There were no police reports. The children—ages six and eight—mentioned that Daddy's 'juice' made him sleepy, but those statements alone were insufficient for court-ordered testing. Then Brian was arrested for DUI on a Saturday evening with both children in the car. His blood alcohol level was 0.14—nearly twice the legal limit. The children were uninjured but had been in the vehicle. Child protective services was called. Allison's attorney filed an emergency motion Monday morning. By Wednesday, Brian's overnights were suspended, Soberlink monitoring was ordered for any future parenting time, and the court directed Brian to complete a substance abuse evaluation before unsupervised contact could resume. Brian's attorney argued the DUI was an isolated incident. The judge reviewed Allison's incident log—eighteen entries over two years documenting the children's reports, Brian's slurred speech at exchanges, and three occasions where Brian failed to pick up the children at the scheduled time without explanation. The DUI was not isolated. It was the documented culmination of a pattern that the court now had independent verification for.

Testing Modalities

Urine testing detects most substances within a window of two to five days. It is the most common form of court-ordered testing but is easily defeated by abstaining for a short period before a scheduled test. Random testing eliminates this vulnerability.

Hair follicle testing provides a detection window of approximately ninety days and is extremely difficult to defeat. It reveals patterns of use rather than single incidents and is increasingly requested in contested custody cases.

EtG (ethyl glucuronide) testing detects alcohol metabolites for approximately eighty hours after consumption—far longer than standard breathalyzer or blood alcohol testing. Useful for monitoring sobriety during parenting time.

Soberlink is a portable breathalyzer with facial recognition and GPS that transmits results to the court, attorneys, and the other parent in real time. Courts order Soberlink monitoring with increasing frequency because it provides verifiable, tamper-resistant documentation of sobriety during parenting time.

SCRAM (Secure Continuous Remote Alcohol Monitor) is an ankle bracelet that continuously monitors alcohol consumption through transdermal detection. It is used in more serious cases and provides twenty-four-hour monitoring.

✦ ✦ ✦

If You Are Managing a Substance Use Issue

If you are the parent with a substance use history—whether active or in recovery—the worst thing you can do is deny, minimize, or conceal. Courts respond to demonstrated recovery with respect. They respond to denial with alarm.

- Acknowledge the issue honestly. A parent who says "I developed a problem, I recognized it, and I have been in treatment for eight months" earns judicial trust.

- Engage in treatment proactively—before the court orders it. Voluntary treatment demonstrates insight. Court-ordered treatment demonstrates compliance.

- Comply with testing without objection. Consistent clean results over time build a powerful record.

- Maintain documentation of your recovery: attendance records, sponsor communications, completion certificates, and therapist notes.

- If you relapse, address it immediately and transparently. A relapse handled with honesty and a return to treatment is recoverable. A relapse concealed and then discovered is devastating.

Courts do not expect perfection. They expect honesty, effort, and sustained commitment to change. The parent who demonstrates all three can rebuild their custody position even after serious substance abuse.

> **Core Principle:** *Courts respect demonstrated recovery. They do not respect denial, minimization, or concealment. If substance abuse is part of your case—on either side—the evidence, not the emotion, determines the outcome.*

CHAPTER 28

Mental Health Issues in Divorce

Mental health intersects with every dimension of divorce—custody, credibility, financial claims, judicial perception, and the daily capacity to withstand the most stressful legal process most people will ever face. This chapter addresses both sides: when your spouse's mental health is the concern, and when yours is.

When Your Spouse's Mental Health Is the Issue

A spouse's untreated or poorly managed mental illness can affect parenting capacity, judgment, emotional regulation, and the safety of the household. Courts evaluate the functional impact of mental health conditions—not the diagnosis itself. Depression that is treated and managed is not a custody concern. Depression that is untreated and produces prolonged inability to meet a child's basic needs is a legitimate concern.

Document the impact, not the label:

- Specific incidents where the condition affected parenting: missed school pickups, inability to get out of bed for extended periods, erratic behavior witnessed by the children

- Records from professionals who have observed the impact: therapist notes, pediatrician observations, school counselor concerns

- Communications that reveal instability: incoherent messages, rapid mood shifts documented in text exchanges, threats of self-harm used as manipulation

- Patterns over time: a single bad day is not a custody concern. A pattern of dysregulation across months is.

Avoid amateur diagnosis. Telling the court "My spouse has borderline personality disorder" without a clinical evaluation to support it damages your credibility. Describe the behavior. Let the professionals apply the labels.

When You Are Managing Mental Health Challenges

If you are living with depression, anxiety, PTSD, bipolar disorder, or any other mental health condition, the worst thing you can do is hide it. Courts do not penalize parents for having mental health conditions. They penalize parents for refusing to acknowledge or address them.

- Engage in consistent treatment. Therapy attendance, medication compliance, and psychiatric follow-through are evidence of responsibility and self-awareness.

- Maintain a record of your treatment. Appointment logs, prescription records, and therapist letters documenting your progress are powerful evidence that you are managing your condition.

- Be transparent with the evaluator. An evaluator who discovers a concealed diagnosis trusts you less than one who hears you say: "I was diagnosed with bipolar II three years ago. I take lithium daily, see my psychiatrist monthly, and my therapist weekly. My condition is stable and well managed."

- Acknowledge the impact on your parenting honestly. "There were months where my depression made me less present than I wanted to be. I recognized that, sought treatment, and have been consistent since" earns respect.

WHAT I'VE SEEN: The Diagnosis That Helped Her Case

Olivia disclosed her bipolar II diagnosis to the custody evaluator before the evaluator asked about it. She brought three years of psychiatric records showing consistent lithium levels, monthly appointments, and no hospitalizations. She described the period before diagnosis—the mood episodes that had strained the marriage—with candor and without deflection. She explained what she had learned, what her warning signs were, and what her crisis plan involved if she experienced a breakthrough episode. The evaluator noted Olivia's 'exceptional insight into her condition and a demonstrated capacity for sustained self-management.' Olivia's ex-husband's attorney had planned to use the diagnosis as the centerpiece of his custody argument. Instead, the evaluator's report treated Olivia's mental health management as evidence of her maturity, her commitment to her children's stability, and her willingness to do difficult personal work. The diagnosis that her ex-husband expected would disqualify her became evidence that qualified her.

Court-Ordered Psychological Evaluations

In contested custody cases, the court may order one or both parents to undergo psychological testing. Common instruments include the MMPI-2 (Minnesota Multiphasic Personality Inventory), the MCMI-IV (Millon Clinical Multiaxial Inventory), and parenting-specific assessments. These tests are designed to detect exaggeration, minimization, and deception—and they are remarkably effective at it.

Do not attempt to game psychological testing. Test instruments contain validity scales specifically calibrated to identify attempts at impression management. A parent who tries to appear "too good"—answering every question as though they have never experienced a negative thought—triggers the same red flags as a parent who exaggerates pathology. Answer honestly. The tests work best, and produce the most favorable results, when the person taking them tells the truth.

Therapists as Witnesses

Therapy records are not automatically confidential in custody litigation. Depending on your jurisdiction, records may be discoverable if mental health has been placed at issue in the case—either by your own claims or by the other party's allegations. A therapist may be compelled to testify about their observations, their clinical impressions, and the content of sessions.

Before you begin therapy, understand the limits of confidentiality in your jurisdiction. Choose a therapist who is experienced with high-conflict divorce and who documents sessions in a manner that reflects careful, clinical observation rather than casual conversation. What your therapist writes in their notes may eventually be read by a judge.

> **Core Principle:** *Mental health challenges do not disqualify you as a parent or diminish your right to custody. Refusing to acknowledge or address them might. The parent who confronts the issue honestly, engages in treatment, and demonstrates sustained management earns judicial respect—not sympathy, but respect.*

CHAPTER 29

Parental Alienation — When Your Child Is Turned Against You

There is a particular agony in watching your child pull away from you—not because of something you did, but because of something the other parent is doing. Your child repeats phrases that sound scripted. They use language no child their age would produce independently. They recite a catalog of grievances that mirrors, almost word for word, the other parent's narrative. Their rejection of you is sudden, absolute, and resistant to evidence or reason.

This is parental alienation—the deliberate campaign by one parent to undermine, damage, or destroy the child's relationship with the other parent. It is real. It is identifiable. And when documented properly, courts address it. But the pathway to proving alienation is narrow, and the consequences of pursuing it poorly are severe.

Alienation vs. Estrangement

The first and most important distinction: not every child who resists contact with a parent has been alienated. Some children have legitimate reasons for their reluctance—they were exposed to violence, they witnessed behavior that frightened them, or they were neglected in ways that damaged trust. This is estrangement, and it is the child's authentic response to their own experience.

Courts and evaluators distinguish between the two by examining the proportionality and specificity of the child's rejection. An alienated child typically rejects the targeted parent completely, without nuance, and cannot articulate specific, credible reasons for the rejection beyond vague, borrowed phrases. An estranged child typically has specific, detailed memories of concerning behavior and may still express ambivalence or love alongside their resistance.

Filing an alienation claim when the child's rejection is actually estrangement—based on your own behavior—is one of the most damaging mistakes a parent can make. It tells the court you lack insight into the impact of your conduct on your child.

Warning Signs of an Alienation Campaign

- The child's rejection is sudden, absolute, and disproportionate to anything that actually occurred between you and the child

- The child uses adult language, legal terminology, or phrases that mirror the other parent's communications

- The child claims to have independently decided to reject you but cannot provide specific, credible reasons

- The other parent "supports" the child's rejection rather than encouraging the relationship—"I can't force them to go. They're old enough to decide."

- The child expresses hatred or contempt that bears no relationship to their prior bond with you

- Extended family on the alienating parent's side also rejects or excludes you without independent reason

- The child has been exposed to court documents, adult communications, or details about the case that no child should possess

- The alienating parent interferes with phone calls, cancels visits, schedules conflicting activities during your parenting time, or creates conditions that make visits uncomfortable for the child

---

WHAT I'VE SEEN: The Campaign That Took Eighteen Months to Prove

---

For eighteen months after separation, Derek's ten-year-old son, Ethan, progressively refused contact. Ethan had been close to Derek throughout his childhood—camping trips, baseball games, nightly bedtime reading. After the separation, Ethan's mother, Jennifer, began a sustained campaign. She told Ethan that Derek 'chose to leave the family.' She cried in front of him after exchanges. She scheduled birthday parties and playdates during Derek's parenting weekends, then told Ethan that Derek was 'keeping him from his friends.' She showed Ethan financial documents and told him Derek was 'taking money from the family.' By month twelve, Ethan refused to get in Derek's car. By month fifteen, he told the therapist that Derek was 'a bad person who hurt our family.' Derek's attorney documented the pattern: the timing of each refusal correlated with Jennifer's interference. The therapist's notes showed Ethan using phrases identical to Jennifer's text messages. School records showed Ethan's grades dropping during the alienation period. A forensic psychologist evaluated the family and concluded that Ethan's rejection was 'not consistent with any experience of abuse, neglect, or legitimate concern, but rather reflects the systematic influence of the custodial parent.' The court ordered a reunification therapy program and modified custody to give Derek increased parenting time with therapeutic support. Jennifer was warned that continued interference would result in a custody transfer. The case took eighteen months to prove because alienation requires pattern evidence, not a single incident. Derek's meticulous documentation—every canceled visit, every scripted phrase, every correlated timeline—built the record that saved the relationship.

Documenting Alienation Without Making It Worse

- Maintain a detailed log of every incident: refused visits, canceled calls, scripted statements, interference with scheduled time

- Save all communications with the other parent that reveal the pattern—scheduling conflicts created deliberately, hostile messages, and statements that reveal the campaign

- Record your child's exact words when they refuse contact or repeat the other parent's narrative—use their language, not your interpretation

- Continue reaching out to your child consistently. Send messages, letters, and invitations to events. Document every effort. A parent who gives up provides evidence that they abandoned the relationship.

- Do not criticize the alienating parent to the child, interrogate the child about the campaign, or place the child in a position of choosing sides. You must remain the parent who does not pull the child into the conflict—even when the other parent is doing exactly that.

Working with Professionals

Alienation claims require professional support. A therapist experienced in high-conflict family dynamics can identify and document the pattern. A forensic psychologist can evaluate the family and provide expert testimony. A guardian ad litem can investigate independently and advocate for the child's authentic interests.

Choose professionals carefully. A therapist who immediately validates your alienation claim without independent assessment may lack the credibility courts require. A professional who examines the evidence thoroughly, considers alternative explanations, and reaches a supported conclusion carries far more weight.

How Weak Alienation Claims Backfire

A parent who files an alienation claim that the evidence does not support damages their own case. The court concludes that the parent lacks insight into why the child resists contact. The parent is seen as blaming the other side rather than examining their own behavior. And the claim itself becomes ammunition for the opposing attorney: "This parent refuses to accept responsibility for the deterioration of their own relationship with their child."

Before filing an alienation claim, ask yourself—and your attorney—two questions: Is there a documented pattern of alienating behavior by the other parent? And have I honestly examined whether my own behavior contributed to the child's resistance? If the answer to the first question is yes and the second is no, pursue the claim. If there is any doubt, seek a professional evaluation before committing to the alienation framework.

Core Principle: *The strongest evidence of alienation is a documented pattern over time—not a single incident or an emotional accusation. Build the record patiently. Remain the parent who does not pull the child into the war. And let the professionals connect the evidence to the conclusion.*

COMPANION VOLUME — For the comprehensive alienation strategy guide—including reunification therapy protocols, advanced documentation techniques, and detailed courtroom presentation strategies—see companion volume Chapter 12.

Disciplined use of professionals—each in their proper role—maximizes the return on every dollar spent and prevents costly strategic errors.

PART VIII

YOUR LEGAL TEAM, PROFESSIONALS, AND WORKING THE SYSTEM

Divorce is not a solo operation. The outcome of your case will be shaped by the professionals you choose to work with—your attorney, your financial experts, your therapist, your mediator—and by how effectively you work with them. The five chapters ahead address every professional relationship that matters: how to select the right people, how to communicate with them productively, how to control costs without sacrificing quality, and how to recognize when you have the wrong team.

CHAPTER 30

Choosing and Working with Your Divorce Lawyer

Your attorney is the single most consequential hiring decision you will make during this process. A good divorce lawyer shortens the case, reduces the cost, identifies risks you cannot see, and positions you for the best outcome the facts permit. A bad one generates unnecessary conflict, misses deadlines, fails to prepare, and bills you for the privilege.

The selection process deserves the same rigor you would apply to hiring a surgeon. Both perform operations with lasting consequences. Both require specialized experience. And both should be evaluated on track record, not personality alone.

How to Find the Right Attorney

Begin with referrals from people whose judgment you trust—friends, family members, or colleagues who have been through divorce and were satisfied with their representation. If you know any attorneys personally, ask for a family law referral; lawyers know which practitioners in their community are competent and which are not. Your state bar association's lawyer referral service can provide names, though the quality varies.

Once you have three to five names, research each one. Review their website for specialization in family law—not general practice with family law as one item on a long list. Check for disciplinary history through your state bar's online database. Read online reviews with intelligence: a single angry review from an opposing party means nothing; a pattern of complaints about poor communication or missed deadlines means everything.

The Consultation: What to Ask

Most family law attorneys offer an initial consultation—often thirty to sixty minutes, sometimes at a reduced fee. This meeting is a two-way interview. You are evaluating the attorney as much as they are evaluating your case.

- How long have you practiced family law exclusively? Five years is a minimum. Ten or more is preferable for contested cases.

- How many cases have you taken to trial? An attorney who has never tried a case cannot credibly threaten trial during negotiations—and opposing counsel knows it.

- What is your approach to this type of case? Listen for strategy, not aggression. An attorney who promises to "destroy" your spouse is selling emotion, not competence.

- How will you communicate with me? Weekly updates? Email responsiveness within twenty-four hours? Monthly billing summaries? Clear expectations prevent expensive misunderstandings.

- Who will actually work on my case? In larger firms, the partner you meet may delegate the daily work to an associate. Know who will handle hearings, draft motions, and return your calls.

- What is your fee structure, and what should I expect this case to cost? No attorney can give a precise number, but an experienced one can provide a realistic range based on the complexity you describe.

Fee Structures

Hourly billing is the standard in contested divorce. You pay for the attorney's time at a defined rate—commonly $250 to $600 per hour depending on the market and the attorney's experience. A retainer (typically $5,000 to $25,000) is deposited upfront and drawn against as work is performed.

Flat fees are available for straightforward, uncontested divorces where the scope of work is predictable. If your case is genuinely simple—no children, limited assets, mutual agreement on terms—a flat fee can be economical.

Limited-scope representation (also called unbundled services) allows you to hire an attorney for specific tasks—drafting a settlement agreement, reviewing a proposed parenting plan, appearing at a single hearing—rather than full representation. This is a viable option when you can handle some aspects of the case yourself but need professional help on the critical elements.

WHAT I'VE SEEN: The Attorney Who Billed for the War She Started

---

Nathan hired an attorney based on a friend's recommendation and a first meeting that felt reassuring. The attorney was aggressive, confident, and promised to "fight hard." Within three months, Nathan's attorney had filed seven motions—including a motion to compel production of documents Nathan's wife had already provided, a motion for contempt based on a scheduling misunderstanding, and an emergency motion alleging a parenting violation that the court dismissed in under five minutes. Each motion required preparation, filing, a hearing, and opposing counsel's response. Nathan's legal bill *reached $47,000 in four months. His case was no closer to resolution. The opposing attorney told Nathan's wife's attorney that she dreaded every filing because 'nothing in these motions is substantive.' Nathan changed lawyers. His new attorney reviewed the file, withdrew the pending motions, and resolved the case through mediation in six weeks for $8,200 in additional fees. The first attorney had generated $47,000 in bills by manufacturing conflict. The second attorney resolved the case for a fraction of that amount by addressing the actual issues. Nathan's mistake was not hiring a lawyer. It was hiring a lawyer who profited from prolonging the fight.*

Controlling Legal Costs

- Organize before you communicate. Send one structured email rather than five separate texts. Your attorney bills for every interaction—including the time spent reading, processing, and responding to scattered messages.

- Prepare for every meeting with a written agenda and bring all relevant documents. An hour with a prepared client produces three times the strategic value of an hour spent sorting through disorganized concerns.

- Reserve your attorney for legal matters. Your therapist handles the emotional processing. Your attorney handles the legal strategy. Confusing those roles costs $300 to $500 per hour in misdirected billing.

- Respond to discovery requests promptly and completely. Delays generate follow-up letters, motions to compel, and hearings—all billable, all avoidable.

- Ask for monthly itemized billing statements and review them. Errors happen. Overbilling happens. An informed client catches both.

When to Change Lawyers

Changing attorneys mid-case is disruptive and expensive—the new attorney must review the entire file, learn the history, and establish relationships with opposing counsel and the court. It should not be done lightly. But it should be done when the situation demands it.

- Your attorney is not returning calls or emails for days at a time, consistently.

- Deadlines are being missed or filings contain errors that a competent practitioner would catch.

- Your attorney appears unprepared at hearings—unfamiliar with the facts, unable to answer the judge's questions.

- The case is generating conflict and expense with no strategic justification.

- You have lost confidence in the attorney's competence or judgment, and that confidence cannot be restored.

If you change lawyers, do it cleanly. Notify your current attorney in writing, request a full copy of your file, and ensure a smooth hand-off to your new counsel. Do not leave gaps in representation during active litigation.

Core Principle: *Your attorney is a strategic partner—not a therapist, not a magician, and not a weapon. The quality of your collaboration determines the quality of your outcome.*

CHAPTER 31

Financial Professionals — CPAs, Forensic Accountants, and Financial Advisors

In financially complex divorces, the financial professionals may determine your outcome as much as the attorneys. A CPA who identifies a $30,000 tax liability that your spouse's settlement proposal ignores saves you $30,000. A forensic accountant who uncovers $150,000 in hidden business income changes the entire support calculation. A Certified Divorce Financial Analyst who models the next twenty years of your post-divorce financial life reveals whether a proposed settlement leaves you solvent or slowly broke.

When You Need a CPA

Every divorce with meaningful assets or income should involve a tax professional—if only for a targeted review of the settlement's tax consequences. Common issues that require CPA involvement:

- The tax implications of selling the marital home: capital gains exclusions, basis calculations, and the timing of the sale relative to the divorce

- Filing status in the year of divorce: married filing jointly vs. separately, and how the choice affects total tax liability

- Dependency exemptions and child tax credits: which parent claims which child, and the financial impact of the allocation

- Tax treatment of retirement account transfers: QDRO-facilitated transfers are tax-neutral; improper transfers trigger penalties and withholding

- Alimony tax treatment for pre-2019 agreements: modification may inadvertently change the tax characterization

When You Need a Forensic Accountant

A forensic accountant is an investigator, not a tax preparer. Engage one when:

- Your spouse owns or controls a business, and income or asset values are disputed

- Lifestyle does not match reported income—the family spends $180,000 annually, but tax returns show $95,000

- You suspect assets have been hidden, transferred, or undervalued

- Large cash withdrawals, new entities, or unexplained transfers appear in the financial records

- Your spouse is self-employed and controls the books

WHAT I'VE SEEN: The $7,500 That Saved $140,000

Pamela's husband, Russell, owned three fast-food franchise locations. Russell's attorney presented business valuations totaling $410,000 across the three locations. Pamela's attorney recommended engaging a forensic accountant—a $7,500 expense that Pamela hesitated to approve. The forensic accountant examined five years of *tax returns, bank statements for all business and personal accounts, franchise disclosure documents, and industry benchmarks for comparable franchise operations. The analysis revealed that Russell had been running personal expenses through the businesses—$38,000 in vehicle payments, $22,000 in travel, $15,000 in home improvement supplies purchased through the business accounts—reducing reported profit and suppressing the business valuations. After normalizing earnings, the forensic accountant valued the three locations at $690,000. Pamela's share of the marital estate increased by approximately $140,000 as a result. The $7,500 forensic fee produced a return of nearly nineteen to one.*

Certified Divorce Financial Analysts (CDFAs)

A CDFA performs long-term financial modeling—projecting how a proposed settlement will perform over five, ten, and twenty years. Two settlements that appear similar on paper can produce vastly different outcomes over time: one may leave you financially stable at sixty-five; the other may leave you depleted by fifty-five. A CDFA models the impact of inflation, investment returns, Social Security timing, health care costs, and the tax consequences of withdrawing from different account types at different ages.

Engaging a CDFA is particularly valuable when you are choosing between different combinations of assets and support—for example, whether to take the house or a larger share of retirement accounts, whether to accept a lump sum or monthly support, or whether a proposed step-down schedule leaves you viable when the payments end.

> **Core Principle:** *In financially complex divorces, the financial professionals may matter as much as the lawyers. Skipping this investment to save money in the short term often costs far more in the long term.*

CHAPTER 32

Mental Health and Substance Abuse Professionals

Your therapist may be the most important member of your team who never steps inside the courtroom. Individual therapy provides the emotional support that sustains you through the process, gives you a space to process anger and grief without burdening your children or your attorney, and demonstrates to the court that you take your emotional health seriously. Child therapy protects your children from the damage that divorce conflict inflicts. And substance abuse professionals can rebuild the credibility that addiction destroys.

Choosing a Therapist During Divorce

Not every therapist is equipped for the specific demands of high-conflict divorce. Seek a practitioner who:

- Has experience with family law cases and understands that their notes may be reviewed by attorneys, evaluators, or judges

- Focuses on practical coping strategies and emotional regulation rather than extended exploration of childhood trauma—you need tools for the present crisis, not a five-year retrospective

- Documents sessions carefully and clinically, aware that their records may become evidence

- Maintains clear boundaries between the therapeutic role and the forensic role—your therapist advocates for your emotional well-being, not for a specific custody outcome

The Therapeutic Role vs. the Forensic Role

This distinction is critical and widely misunderstood. A treating therapist serves the client's therapeutic needs. They listen, support, advise, and treat. A forensic evaluator serves the court. They assess, test, investigate, and render opinions about custody, fitness, and parenting capacity.

Asking your treating therapist to testify as a forensic expert—to tell the court that you are the better parent or that your spouse is unfit—puts the therapist in an untenable position and frequently backfires. The therapist has heard only your perspective. They have not evaluated the other parent. Their opinion, offered without the rigor of a forensic evaluation, is attacked on cross-examination and often dismissed. Worse, it can cost you the therapist's continued treatment if the therapeutic relationship is compromised by the adversarial role.

Child Therapy

If your child is showing signs of stress during the divorce—behavioral changes, sleep disturbance, academic decline, emotional withdrawal, or regression—therapy provides a safe space for them to process what they are experiencing. A skilled child therapist helps the child understand that the divorce is not their fault, develops coping strategies appropriate to the child's age, and gives you and the court a professional assessment of how the child is functioning.

Both parents typically must consent to therapy for a child unless one parent has sole legal custody or the court orders treatment. If your co-parent refuses to consent, your attorney can petition the court for an order authorizing therapy. Do not delay seeking treatment because your co-parent is obstructing—document the obstruction and pursue a court order.

Parenting Coordinators

A parenting coordinator is a neutral professional—usually a therapist or attorney with family law experience—appointed to resolve day-to-day disputes between high-conflict co-parents. Unlike a mediator, a parenting coordinator can make binding decisions on minor issues: schedule adjustments, holiday conflicts, extracurricular enrollment disagreements, and communication breakdowns.

Parenting coordinators reduce litigation by giving both parents a mechanism to resolve disputes without filing motions. In cases where every scheduling conflict triggers a $2,000 legal skirmish, a parenting coordinator at $200 per hour resolves the same dispute in a single session. Courts order parenting coordinators with increasing frequency, and experienced family law judges view the request favorably.

WHAT I'VE SEEN: The Therapist Who Became a Liability

Kevin's therapist had been treating him for eight months when Kevin's attorney asked her to submit a letter to the court stating that Kevin was 'an excellent father' and that his wife's allegations of emotional instability were unfounded. The therapist, wanting to support her client, drafted a two-page letter opining that Kevin was a devoted parent and that his wife appeared to be 'engaging in parental alienation.' At the hearing, the wife's attorney cross-examined the therapist and asked three questions: Had she ever met the wife? Had she conducted any formal evaluation of the wife's parenting?

Had she interviewed the children? The answer to all three was no. The judge struck the therapist's letter from evidence and noted in the record that it reflected 'advocacy rather than clinical assessment.' Kevin's attempt to turn his treating therapist into a forensic witness accomplished nothing except damaging the therapist's standing with the court and signaling that Kevin's team was willing to stretch professional boundaries to win. The letter that was supposed to help his case became an exhibit that hurt it.

Core Principle: *Engaging professional help is a sign of strength that courts respect. Avoiding it suggests denial that courts penalize. Build your team deliberately, use each professional within their proper role, and let their expertise speak through the process.*

CHAPTER 33

Mediation, Collaborative Divorce, and Alternative Resolution

The vast majority of divorce cases settle before trial. The question is not whether your case will settle, but how—and on whose terms. Mediation, collaborative practice, and other alternative resolution methods give you a role in shaping the outcome. Trial gives that role to a judge who has spent hours with your case while you have spent years living it.

◆ ◆ ◆

Mediation: How It Works

A mediator is a neutral third party who facilitates negotiation between the divorcing spouses. The mediator does not decide the case. They do not issue orders. They help both parties identify areas of agreement, work through impasses, and construct a settlement that both sides can accept.

Facilitative Mediation

The mediator guides the conversation, asks clarifying questions, and helps both parties generate options. The mediator does not offer opinions about what a court would likely decide. This approach works well when both parties are willing to negotiate in good faith and have relatively equal bargaining power.

Evaluative Mediation

The mediator provides an assessment of each party's legal position—essentially telling both sides what a judge would likely do if the case went to trial. Evaluative mediation is effective when one or both parties have unrealistic expectations. Hearing a neutral professional say "Your position on this issue is unlikely to succeed at trial" carries more weight than hearing it from your spouse's attorney.

Preparing for Mediation

Unprepared parties get outmaneuvered in mediation.
Preparation means:

- Defining your priorities in advance: what are the three or four outcomes that matter most? What are you willing to concede?

- Knowing the numbers: current account balances, property values, income figures, monthly expenses, debt balances. Arriving without financial clarity gives the better-informed spouse an advantage.

- Understanding your legal position: what would a court likely order if mediation fails? Your attorney should brief you on probable outcomes so you can evaluate proposals against the realistic alternative.

- Identifying your walk-away point: the minimum acceptable outcome below which you would rather take your chances at trial

- Organizing your documentation: bring supporting documents for every contested issue—appraisals, pay stubs, expense worksheets, proposed parenting schedules

---

WHAT I'VE SEEN: The Mediation That Saved the Family $94,000

Andrea and Philip had been preparing for trial—combined legal fees already exceeded $56,000, and their attorneys estimated trial preparation and a three-day hearing would cost another $40,000 to $50,000 each. Their attorneys suggested a final attempt at mediation before a retired family court judge serving as an evaluative mediator. Andrea arrived with a one-page summary of her priorities, a detailed expense worksheet, and a proposed parenting schedule with three alternative configurations. Philip arrived with a spreadsheet showing five settlement scenarios with different combinations of the house, the retirement accounts, and the support obligation. The mediator spent three hours shuttling between rooms. By the end of the session, Andrea and Philip had agreed on a parenting plan, a property division, and a three-year rehabilitative alimony arrangement. Total mediation cost: $2,400 split between them. The settlement was imperfect—neither party received everything they wanted. But both received outcomes within the range of what a judge would likely have ordered, without the additional $94,000 in combined legal fees that trial would have consumed. Their children never sat in a courthouse hallway. Neither parent testified against the other. The case ended with a handshake and a signed agreement.

When Mediation Is Inappropriate

Mediation assumes a roughly equal negotiating position between the parties. When that assumption fails, mediation can produce outcomes that are unfair to the disadvantaged party:

- Active domestic violence: a victim sitting across from their abuser—even in separate rooms—may concede out of fear rather than informed choice

- Significant power imbalances: when one spouse controlled all financial information and the other has no independent knowledge of the family's assets

- Active substance abuse or untreated mental illness that impairs one party's capacity to negotiate

- A spouse who negotiates in bad faith—using mediation to delay, to gather information, or to create the appearance of good faith while having no intention of reaching agreement

Collaborative Divorce

In collaborative practice, each spouse retains a specially trained collaborative attorney, and both parties sign an agreement committing to resolve the case outside of court. The distinguishing feature—and the primary risk—is the disqualification provision: if the collaborative process fails and the case proceeds to litigation, both collaborative attorneys are disqualified and each party must hire new counsel.

This provision creates a powerful incentive for both sides to reach agreement. It also creates a significant financial risk: if the process collapses after months of negotiation, you have paid for an attorney you can no longer use and must now pay a second attorney to start over. Collaborative divorce works best when both parties are genuinely committed to settlement and have the emotional capacity for constructive negotiation. It is poorly suited for high-conflict personalities who will exploit the no-court commitment as a shield against accountability.

Arbitration

In arbitration, a private decision-maker—usually a retired judge or experienced family law attorney—hears the case and issues a binding or non-binding decision. Arbitration offers the advantage of speed, privacy, and the ability to choose your decision-maker. It lacks the ability to appeal in most binding arbitration agreements, which means you are committed to the arbitrator's judgment.

The Art of Settlement Negotiation

Whether in mediation, collaborative practice, or direct attorney-to-attorney negotiation, the principles of effective settlement are consistent:

- Anchor with your first offer. Research consistently shows that the first number proposed shapes the range of negotiation. Start with a reasonable but favorable position.

- Concede strategically. Every concession should be exchanged for something of value. "I'll agree to alternating holidays if you agree to the 5-2-2-5 schedule during the school year."

- Separate the people from the problem. Your spouse's behavior during the marriage is not the subject of the negotiation. The financial and custodial terms of the divorce are.

- Know when to accept. A settlement that gives you 80 percent of what you wanted at 20 percent of the cost of trial is almost always the right decision.

Core Principle: *Settlement is not surrender. It is strategic resolution on terms you helped design—rather than terms a judge imposed with limited information and limited time.*

CHAPTER 34

Self-Representation — Capabilities and Limitations

You have the legal right to represent yourself in divorce. That right comes with no guarantee that you will achieve a fair outcome, no allowance for mistakes you didn't know you could make, and no safety net when the other side has an attorney who does this every day while you are learning the process in real time.

Self-representation works in a narrow range of cases. Outside that range, it is one of the most expensive decisions a divorcing person can make—not because of what it costs, but because of what it gives away.

When Self-Representation Can Work

- Truly uncontested divorce: both parties agree on all terms, no children or simple custodial arrangement, modest assets, no significant income disparity, and both parties are capable of understanding and completing the required paperwork

- Limited financial complexity: no businesses, no pensions requiring QDROs, no hidden assets, no contested property classification

- Both parties are emotionally stable and able to communicate without hostility
- The jurisdiction provides accessible self-help resources, standardized forms, and procedural guidance for pro se litigants

When Self-Representation Is Dangerous

- Contested custody: the stakes are too high and the evidentiary requirements too complex for someone without legal training
- Significant assets or complex property: business valuation, retirement division, real estate portfolios, and tax consequences require professional analysis
- Domestic violence: the legal protections available—protective orders, supervised visitation, firearms restrictions—require procedural knowledge and strategic presentation
- An opposing party with an attorney: you are at a structural disadvantage that grows with every hearing, every filing, and every negotiation
- Anything involving discovery, depositions, or expert witnesses: the procedural rules are unforgiving, and violations can result in sanctions or adverse rulings

---

WHAT I'VE SEEN: The Agreement She Didn't Understand

Carla and her husband agreed to divorce amicably. Neither hired an attorney. They found a settlement template online and filled it out together at the kitchen table. Carla signed the agreement believing she understood its terms. She did not. The agreement waived her right to spousal support permanently—not for a defined period, but forever. It divided the retirement accounts by naming a dollar amount that had been current six months earlier but was $42,000 below the present value by the time the decree was entered.

It contained no QDRO provision, leaving Carla with no mechanism to collect her share. It assigned Carla the marital home but left her husband's name on the mortgage—giving him no incentive to ensure the payments were made and leaving Carla responsible for a loan she could not refinance on her single income. Three years later, Carla contacted an attorney seeking to modify the agreement. The attorney explained that most of the provisions were non-modifiable: the property division was final, the waiver of support was permanent, and the failure to include a QDRO meant the retirement funds would require a separate legal action to access. Carla's amicable kitchen-table agreement cost her approximately $190,000 in retirement assets, an indefinite support right she could never recover, and a mortgage obligation that eventually forced her to sell the house at a loss. The agreement was free. Its consequences were catastrophic.

How Judges Treat Pro Se Parties

Judges are generally patient with self-represented litigants. They will explain procedures, allow extra time, and tolerate minor errors. But patience has limits. A judge will not:

- Advocate for you or advise you on strategy—the judge must remain neutral

- Excuse your failure to comply with procedural rules that an attorney would have known

- Give you more favorable treatment to compensate for your lack of representation

- Overlook missed deadlines, improperly formatted filings, or inadequate evidence

The legal system holds self-represented parties to the same substantive standards as represented parties. You may receive procedural patience, but you will not receive a different legal standard.

The Strategic Middle Ground: Limited-Scope Representation

If full representation is beyond your budget but self-representation exposes you to unacceptable risk, limited-scope representation offers a middle path. You handle the day-to-day aspects of the case—attending hearings, filing routine documents, communicating with your spouse—while an attorney provides targeted assistance on the critical elements:

- Reviewing and negotiating the settlement agreement before you sign it

- Preparing you for your testimony and key hearings

- Drafting the QDRO and ensuring retirement accounts are properly divided

- Advising on complex property or custody issues where the legal analysis exceeds your capacity

- Reviewing your spouse's proposed parenting plan for provisions that disadvantage you

Limited-scope representation costs a fraction of full representation—often $2,000 to $5,000 for targeted work—and addresses the highest-risk elements of your case while leaving the routine work in your hands.

Resources for Self-Represented Litigants

- Your courthouse's self-help center: many courts maintain offices specifically to assist pro se litigants with forms, procedures, and filing requirements

- Legal aid organizations: income-qualified individuals may receive free or reduced-fee representation for divorce matters

- Law school family law clinics: supervised law students provide representation under attorney oversight, often at no cost

- State bar referral services: may offer initial consultations at reduced fees

- Online legal platforms (with extreme caution): document preparation services can generate basic forms, but they do not provide legal advice, do not account for your specific circumstances, and bear no responsibility for the consequences of an inadequate agreement

Core Principle: *Self-representation is a legal right. Understanding its risks and limitations is a strategic responsibility. If you proceed without an attorney, do so with your eyes open—and at minimum, have a professional review the final agreement before you sign it.*

The courtroom is where credibility is tested under fire. Everything you have built converges in your testimony

PART IX

THE COURTROOM: HEARINGS, TRIAL, AND TESTIMONY

Most divorce cases settle. But every case must be prepared as if it will not. The three chapters ahead address the highest-stakes moments in the process—walking into a courtroom, taking the witness stand, and what happens after the judge signs the decree. Trials are won in the weeks of preparation that precede them, not in the moment of performance.

CHAPTER 35

Preparing for Hearings and Trial

A courtroom is not a conversation. It is a structured proceeding governed by rules of evidence, rules of procedure, and the temperament of a judge who has forty-seven other cases on the docket this month. Your preparation determines whether those rules work for you or against you.

Types of Hearings

Temporary orders hearings occur early in the case. They establish interim custody, support, exclusive possession of the home, and restraining provisions while the divorce is pending. Temporary orders shape the status quo—and as you learned in Chapter 10, the status quo has gravitational force. Treat these hearings with the same seriousness as a final trial.

Contested motion hearings resolve specific disputes: discovery violations, contempt allegations, requests to modify temporary orders, or protective order proceedings. They are typically shorter than trial—thirty minutes to two hours—and may be decided without full evidentiary presentation.

Final trial is the full evidentiary hearing where the court determines custody, property division, support, and all remaining contested issues. Trials in family law cases typically last one to five days, though complex cases can extend longer.

What Judges Prioritize

Family court judges make high-consequence decisions under time pressure. They value:

- Concise, organized presentation. A judge who must sift through disorganized evidence is a judge whose patience is depleted before your strongest points are reached.

- Factual testimony over emotional testimony. The parent who says 'On October 14, the children reported they had not eaten dinner and the house was in disarray' is more persuasive than the parent who says 'He's a terrible father who doesn't care about the kids.'

- Evidence that speaks for itself. Text messages, financial records, photographs, and professional reports carry more weight than one spouse's characterization of the other.

- Proportionality. A party who brings five witnesses and forty exhibits to a temporary hearing over a scheduling dispute signals poor judgment about resource allocation.

Preparing Your Testimony

- Meet with your attorney to outline the key points your testimony must cover. Know your narrative arc—beginning, middle, and the specific outcome you are requesting.

- Anticipate opposing counsel's attacks. What are the weakest points in your case? What will the other side highlight? Prepare honest, composed responses.

- Practice answering questions aloud. Hearing yourself speak the words reveals where your answers are too long, too emotional, or insufficiently specific.

- Review every document that may be referenced during your testimony. If it is in evidence, you should know what it says before opposing counsel shows it to you on the stand.

Physical Presentation

- Dress as you would for a professional job interview. Conservative. Clean. Unremarkable. The goal is to be noticed for your testimony, not your appearance.

- Arrive early. Rushing into a courtroom flustered undermines the composure you need on the stand.

- Sit upright, hands visible, face toward whoever is speaking. Do not roll your eyes, shake your head, or react visibly to opposing testimony. The judge is watching you even when you are not testifying.

- Bring water but not food. Silence your phone completely. Have documents organized and tabbed so you can locate anything your attorney requests without fumbling.

WHAT I'VE SEEN: The Five Minutes That Decided the Trial

Both parents were competent. Both loved their children. The evidence on paper was closely matched. The trial was expected to last three days. On the morning of Day 1, Anthony's attorney called him to the stand first. Anthony spoke clearly, maintained eye contact with the judge, and described his parenting involvement in specific, dated, measurable terms: 'I have attended every parent-teacher conference since 2019. I manage both children's medical appointments, including the ongoing allergy treatment plan with Dr. Sanchez. I prepare dinner five nights a week and supervise homework from 6:30 to 8:00 each evening.' When asked about his wife, he said: 'She is a good mother. My concern is that her work travel—averaging twelve nights per month—leaves the children in inconsistent care arrangements, and I believe a more stable primary home would serve them better.' His wife's attorney cross-examined aggressively, but Anthony remained calm. He corrected inaccurate premises without raising his voice. He said 'I don't recall the specific date, but I can check my records' twice rather than guessing. On rebuttal, his wife's testimony was emotional, reactive, and unfocused. She interrupted opposing counsel twice and directed a comment to Anthony directly—prompting the judge to admonish her. By the afternoon recess, the judge had seen everything needed. The trial settled before Day 2 began—on terms that closely reflected what Anthony had requested. The first five minutes of Anthony's testimony set a tone that the remaining hours could not overcome.

Core Principle: *Trials are won in the weeks and months of preparation that precede them—not in the moment of performance. The client who has rehearsed composure, organized evidence, and anticipated attacks walks into the courtroom with earned confidence.*

CHAPTER 36

How to Testify with Strength and Credibility

The witness stand is where cases are decided. Your attorney's arguments frame the issues. Your evidence supports the arguments. But your testimony—your voice, your composure, your ability to tell the truth clearly and withstand attack—is what a judge remembers when the courtroom goes quiet and the decision must be made.

The Foundational Rules

- Answer only the question asked. Do not volunteer information. If opposing counsel asks 'Did you attend the school conference on September 12?' the answer is 'Yes.' Not 'Yes, and I also attended every conference since kindergarten and my spouse missed four of them.' Your attorney will draw out favorable details on redirect.

- Tell the truth. Always. A single lie or exaggeration, caught on cross-examination, contaminates everything else you have said. Judges evaluate witnesses through a credibility filter—once the filter is damaged, it cannot be repaired.

- Maintain composure under pressure. Opposing counsel will test you. They will ask provocative questions. They will imply things that are unfair. Your reaction to provocation tells the judge more about your character than any substantive answer.

- Pause before answering. A two-second pause gives your attorney time to object if the question is improper and gives you time to formulate a precise response rather than a reactive one.

Surviving Cross-Examination

Cross-examination is designed to challenge your version of events, expose inconsistencies, and provoke emotional reactions that undermine your believability. The techniques are predictable:

Leading questions. 'Isn't it true that you were out drinking on the night of March 8 while the children were home alone?' The question assumes facts. If the premise is wrong, say so calmly: 'No. I was at a dinner with coworkers. The children were with my mother, who was babysitting at my request.'

False choices. 'So you either forgot your son's medication or you deliberately withheld it?' Reject the false binary: 'Neither. His prescription was being refilled, and I administered it the following morning as soon as the pharmacy opened.'

Emotional provocation. 'You don't really think you're a fit parent, do you?' Do not take the bait. A measured response—'I believe I am a good parent, and I think my record of involvement supports that'— deflates the provocation.

Rapid-fire questioning. Opposing counsel may accelerate the pace, hoping you will answer faster than you can think. Slow down. Take the pause. The judge is not timing your response speed.

Language That Strengthens vs. Language That Destroys

Certain phrases build trust with the court. Others erode it immediately:

- Strong: 'On that specific date, I recall ...' Weak: 'I think maybe it was around that time.'

- Strong: 'I don't recall the exact date. I can review my records.' Weak: 'I don't remember anything about that.'

- Strong: 'That's not accurate. What happened was ...' Weak: 'That's a lie!'

- Strong: 'I made a mistake, and I have addressed it by ...' Weak: 'It wasn't my fault—she provoked me.'

- Strong: 'I believe my spouse is capable in many areas. My concern is specific to ...' Weak: 'He's a terrible person and everyone knows it.'

WHAT I'VE SEEN: The Witness Who Recovered

During cross-examination, Michelle was asked about a text message she had sent to a friend calling her husband 'a sociopath who should never see the kids again.' The message had been produced during discovery. Opposing counsel enlarged it on screen and read it aloud. Michelle's face flushed. She paused for three seconds—long enough to feel like an eternity in the courtroom. Then she said: 'I sent that message during one of the worst nights of my life. It does not reflect my actual belief about my children's relationship with their father. I support their time with him, and my parenting record since that night demonstrates that.' The judge's notes, obtained later during the appeal process, read: 'Mother acknowledged unfavorable text with candor. Response was measured and reflective of growth. Court finds the text inconsistent with her subsequent conduct.' Michelle did not deny the message. She did not attack opposing counsel. She owned the mistake, placed it in context, and pointed to evidence that showed she had moved beyond it. Her three-second pause and honest response transformed a damaging exhibit into a demonstration of maturity.

Core Principle: *The most compelling witness is not the most dramatic or emotional. The most compelling witness is the most believable. Believability is built on specificity, composure, honesty—and the willingness to acknowledge imperfection.*

CHAPTER 37

After Judgment — Enforcement, Modification, and Moving Forward

The judge has signed the decree. The case is over. Except it is not—not if your ex-spouse refuses to comply with the order, not if circumstances change materially, and not in the sense that rebuilding your life after divorce requires deliberate effort that the legal system does not provide.

Understanding Your Final Decree

Read your divorce decree as though it is a contract with enforceable penalties—because it is. Know what it requires you to do, what it requires your ex-spouse to do, and the deadlines attached to each obligation. Common sources of post-judgment conflict include failure to refinance the home within the specified period, missed QDRO filings, late or incomplete property transfers, support payments that begin on a date one party did not notice, and custody provisions that are ambiguous enough to generate disagreement.

If any provision is unclear, ask your attorney to explain it before the decree is signed. Ambiguity in a final order is a motion waiting to be filed.

Enforcement When Your Ex-Spouse Refuses to Comply

- Contempt of court: the primary enforcement mechanism. If your ex-spouse violates a court order—fails to pay support, withholds visitation, refuses to transfer property—you can file a contempt motion asking the court to compel compliance and impose sanctions.

- Wage garnishment: for unpaid support, the court can order the obligor's employer to withhold support directly from wages.

- Property liens: unpaid support or property obligations can be secured by placing a lien on real property, preventing sale or refinancing until the debt is satisfied.

- License suspension: many states authorize suspension of driver's licenses, professional licenses, or recreational licenses for chronic support non-payment.

- Credit reporting: unpaid support can be reported to credit agencies, affecting the obligor's ability to obtain loans, housing, and employment.

Modification

Custody, support, and alimony orders can be modified when a material change in circumstances has occurred since the order was entered. Property division, in most jurisdictions, cannot be modified—it is final. The change must be substantial, involuntary, and ongoing. The process for seeking modification is the same as for the original order: file a motion, present evidence, and demonstrate that the current order no longer serves the interests of justice or the children.

As emphasized throughout this book: if your circumstances change, file promptly. Arrearages accumulate from the date of the existing order, not the date you file for modification.

Appeals

Appeals are expensive, slow, and rarely successful in family law. An appellate court reviews whether the trial judge made a legal error—it does not retry the case or reweigh the evidence. If the trial judge applied the correct legal standard and made findings supported by the evidence, the ruling will be affirmed even if a different judge might have reached a different conclusion.

Discuss the possibility of appeal with your attorney honestly. If there is a genuine legal error, an appeal may be warranted. If you are unhappy with the outcome but the judge followed the law, an appeal will cost you $15,000 to $50,000 and produce the same result.

Rebuilding After the Decree

Financial Reconstruction

- Establish independent credit if you do not have it. Open accounts in your own name. Build a payment history.

- Create a post-divorce budget based on your actual income and expenses—not what you hope to earn or what you received during the marriage.

- Review and update beneficiaries on life insurance policies, retirement accounts, bank accounts, and estate planning documents. Your ex-spouse should no longer be the beneficiary of your 401(k) unless the decree requires it.

- Meet with a financial advisor to recalibrate your retirement timeline and investment strategy based on your new financial reality.

Emotional Recovery

Divorce is a grief process. Even when the marriage needed to end, you are mourning the loss of a shared life, a family structure, and an identity. That grief does not follow a predictable timeline, and it does not resolve simply because the judge signed the decree.

Continue therapy if you have been in treatment. Begin therapy if you have not. The emotional work of divorce does not end with the legal work—it begins a new phase that requires support, patience, and the willingness to rebuild at your own pace.

Co-Parenting Beyond the Courthouse

Your children need both of their parents to succeed at this. The litigation is over. The co-parenting is permanent. Every interaction with your ex-spouse from this point forward either reduces conflict for your children or perpetuates it. Choose reduction. Consistently. Even when the other parent does not.

> **Core Principle:** *The final judgment is not the conclusion of your story. It is the foundation for your next chapter—a chapter you write with the clarity, strength, and hard-earned wisdom that this process has demanded of you.*

These specialized circumstances require all four pillars adapted to unique legal frameworks.

PART X

SPECIAL ISSUES IN MODERN DIVORCE

The five chapters ahead address circumstances that affect specific populations—military families, same-sex couples, blended households, families divided by geography, and parents whose cultural or religious values collide during dissolution. If any of these situations apply to you, the specialized rules and considerations described here may be the most consequential content in this book.

CHAPTER 38

New Partners, Blended Families, and Romantic Relationships During Divorce

You are entitled to a personal life. But during an active divorce, your personal life is not personal—it is evidence. How you handle a new relationship, when you introduce a partner to your children, and how that partner behaves around your family can affect custody evaluations, support calculations, and the judge's perception of your priorities.

✦ ✦ ✦

Timing and the Judicial Lens

Judges are human beings who form impressions. A parent who introduces a new romantic partner to the children before the divorce is finalized—particularly before custody is resolved—risks the appearance that they are prioritizing the new relationship over the children's stability. This perception, whether fair or not, can influence custody outcomes.

The safest approach: do not introduce a new partner to the children until the divorce is finalized and the custody arrangement is settled. If you are in a relationship, keep it separate from your parenting time. Do not allow a new partner to attend exchanges, school events, or children's activities during the pendency of the case.

Morality Clauses and Overnight Guest Provisions

Some parenting plans include morality clauses—provisions that restrict overnight guests of the opposite sex (or any romantic partner) when the children are present. While their enforceability varies by jurisdiction, courts in many states will include them when requested, particularly if the children are young or either parent has demonstrated poor judgment regarding partner introductions.

If your parenting plan contains such a clause, comply with it regardless of whether you consider it reasonable. A violation is a violation—and it hands opposing counsel an exhibit at the next hearing.

WHAT I'VE SEEN: The Boyfriend at the Baseball Game

Four months into a contested custody case, Martin brought his new girlfriend to his eight-year-old son's baseball game. The son had not been introduced to the girlfriend previously. Martin's ex-wife was in the bleachers with the custody evaluator, who had arranged to observe the family in a natural setting. The evaluator watched the son's confusion, noted the girlfriend's proprietary body language, and documented Martin's decision to introduce a new adult into the child's life during an active custody dispute. The evaluator's report stated: 'Father demonstrated a lack of attunement to the child's emotional experience during a period of significant transition.' Martin's attorney estimated that the baseball game incident shifted the evaluator's recommendation by approximately ten to fifteen percentage points in the mother's favor. One after-noon. One poorly timed introduction. A measurable impact on the custody outcome.

Core Principle: *Your personal life affects your legal case. Timing, discretion, and awareness of the judicial lens are not optional during an active divorce.*

CHAPTER 39

Relocation and Long-Distance Divorce Issues

When one parent wants to move—for a new job, to be closer to family, to start fresh—the custody arrangement is thrown into immediate crisis. A move of fifty miles can make an alternating-week schedule impossible. A move across state lines raises jurisdictional questions. A move overseas introduces a web of international law.

Legal Standards for Relocation

Most states require the relocating parent to provide written notice—typically sixty to ninety days—before moving with the children. The non-relocating parent has the right to object. If the parents cannot agree, the court decides based on factors including the reason for the move, the impact on the child's relationship with the non-relocating parent, the child's ties to the current community, and whether a modified schedule can preserve meaningful contact.

Some states presume that relocation is permissible if the primary custodial parent has a legitimate reason for the move. Others place the burden on the moving parent to prove the relocation serves the child's best interests. Know your state's framework before making plans.

Long-Distance Parenting Plans

- Extended time during school breaks rather than alternating weekends: summer vacations of four to six weeks, spring break, and a significant holiday block

- Regular video communication—not as a substitute for in-person contact, but as a bridge between visits

- Transportation cost-sharing spelled out precisely: which parent pays for flights, who accompanies the child, and what happens when schedules conflict

- A built-in review mechanism: the plan is revisited annually or when the child's developmental needs change

Interstate Jurisdiction: The UCCJEA

The Uniform Child Custody Jurisdiction and Enforcement Act (UCCJEA) determines which state has authority to make custody decisions. Generally, the child's home state—the state where the child has lived for the six months immediately preceding the filing—has jurisdiction. Once established, that state retains jurisdiction until neither parent nor the child resides there.

Jurisdiction disputes arise when parents live in different states and both file custody actions. Understanding the UCCJEA prevents the nightmare scenario of competing custody orders from different courts.

Core Principle: *Relocation reshapes every aspect of custody and co-parenting. Plan proactively. Provide proper notice. Propose a workable schedule. And never move with the children before the legal process is complete.*

CHAPTER 40

Cultural, Religious, and Educational Conflicts

When divorcing parents hold different religious beliefs, come from different cultural backgrounds, or disagree fundamentally about how their children should be educated, the court is asked to resolve disputes that have no legal answer—only legal frameworks.

✦ ✦ ✦

Religious Upbringing

Courts cannot prefer one religion over another. They can, however, determine how religious decisions are made when the parents disagree. Typical approaches include assigning religious decision-making to one parent (often the parent who has been the primary religious guide), allowing each parent to practice their own faith during their parenting time without restricting the other, or prohibiting either parent from exposing the child to religious practices that demonstrably cause emotional distress.

The parent who presents their religious involvement as a positive, stable influence in the child's life fares better than the parent who frames religion as a weapon against the other side.

✦ ✦ ✦

Education Disputes

Public vs. private school. Homeschool vs. traditional classroom. Gifted programs. Special education placements. When parents with joint legal custody disagree about education, the court considers the child's academic history, any special needs, the cost of the proposed option and each parent's ability to pay, proximity to each parent's home, and which option provides the most continuity with the child's current academic placement.

> **Core Principle:** *Courts respect sincere, deeply held values. They do not respect values deployed as tactical weapons to gain advantage in custody.*

Military Divorce — Specialized Rules and Protections

Military divorce operates under a dual system—federal military regulations layered on top of state family law. Ignoring the federal layer costs military families benefits and protections they may never recover.

The Servicemembers Civil Relief Act (SCRA)

The SCRA protects active-duty servicemembers from default judgments while deployed or on active duty. If you are serving and have been served with divorce papers, the SCRA entitles you to a stay (postponement) of proceedings for the duration of your active service and up to sixty days thereafter. This protection prevents your spouse from obtaining orders while you are unable to participate in the case.

Military Pension Division

Military retirement pay is divisible in divorce under the Uniformed Services Former Spouses' Protection Act (USFSPA). The 10/10 rule determines whether the former spouse can receive direct payment from the Defense Finance and Accounting Service (DFAS): if the marriage overlapped with at least ten years of creditable military service, DFAS will pay the former spouse's share directly. If the overlap is shorter, the military member pays the former spouse's share directly.

The Survivor Benefit Plan (SBP) is equally important—it provides continued retirement income to the former spouse if the servicemember dies. Without SBP election, the former spouse's share of the military pension terminates upon the servicemember's death. Securing SBP coverage in the divorce decree is critical and frequently overlooked.

BAH, Tricare, and Support Calculations

Basic Allowance for Housing (BAH) is often included in income calculations for child support and alimony. Tricare eligibility for former military spouses follows the 20/20/20 rule: if the marriage lasted at least twenty years, the servicemember served at least twenty years, and the marriage and service overlapped by at least twenty years, the former spouse retains full Tricare benefits. A 20/20/15 overlap provides transitional coverage.

Deployment and Custody

Deployment does not mean loss of custody. Many states have adopted legislation preventing courts from using deployment as a basis for permanent custody modification. Temporary modifications during deployment are common—but the returning servicemember's custody rights must be restored upon return.

Core Principle: *Military divorce operates under its own regulatory framework. Ignoring it forfeits benefits and protections you may never recover. Consult an attorney experienced in military family law.*

CHAPTER 42

Same-Sex Divorce, Unmarried Partners, and Nontraditional Families

Since Obergefell v. Hodges in 2015, same-sex marriages are subject to the same divorce laws as heterosexual marriages in every state. The legal framework for dissolution—property division, support, custody—is identical. But certain issues that arise in same-sex divorce and nontraditional family structures have no exact parallel in conventional family law.

Parentage for Non-Biological Parents

In same-sex marriages, one parent may have a biological connection to the child while the other does not. If the non-biological parent has not legally adopted the child, their parental rights may be vulnerable—particularly in states where parentage laws have not been updated to reflect the reality of same-sex families.

If you are a non-biological parent in a same-sex marriage, confirm that you have legally established parentage through adoption, a parentage order, or the presumption of parentage that arises from marriage in your jurisdiction. Do not assume that being married and raising the child is sufficient—in some states, it is not.

Pre-Obergefell Relationships

Couples who were together for years or decades before marriage was legally available face unique property challenges. Assets acquired during the relationship but before the marriage may be classified as separate property in states that do not recognize the pre-marriage period as a legal partnership. A couple who built a life together for fifteen years before marrying in 2015 may find that only the assets acquired during the three years of legal marriage are divisible.

Unmarried Cohabitants

If you were never married, the dissolution of your relationship is governed by contract law and property law rather than family law. Palimony (support claims by unmarried partners) is recognized in some states and rejected in others. Property acquired during cohabitation is not automatically divisible—ownership depends on title, contribution, and any agreements between the parties.

Custody of children born to unmarried parents is governed by the same best-interest standard as custody in divorce. But parentage must first be established—through acknowledgment, genetic testing, or court order—before custody can be adjudicated.

> **Core Principle:** *Family law is evolving. Your rights depend on understanding where the law stands today in your jurisdiction—not where you assume it stands based on general principles or outdated information.*

This is the operational heart of Pillar 3. The Evidence Ladder provides the framework. These chapters provide the tools.

PART XI

EVIDENCE, DOCUMENTATION, AND BUILDING YOUR CASE

Without credible, organized evidence, the strongest legal arguments collapse. These three chapters teach you what evidence wins cases, how to build your documentary record from day one, and how discovery tools force the truth into the open when your spouse would prefer to keep it hidden.

CHAPTER 43

Evidence That Wins Divorce Cases

Judges decide cases based on evidence—not on which parent is angrier, not on which attorney is louder, and not on assumptions about who is telling the truth. The parent who presents organized, credible, specific evidence wins. The parent who presents emotion, accusation, and generalization loses. This distinction holds across every type of case, every courthouse, and every judge.

Categories of Evidence

Documentary evidence: Tax returns, bank statements, pay stubs, text messages, emails, photographs, medical records, school records, police reports. Documents are the backbone of divorce litigation.

Testimonial evidence: Your testimony and the testimony of witnesses. Personal observation, stated under oath, subject to cross-examination.

Expert evidence: Forensic accountants, appraisers, psychologists, vocational evaluators, and other professionals whose specialized knowledge helps the court understand issues beyond lay comprehension.

Demonstrative evidence: Timelines, charts, summaries, and visual aids that organize complex information for judicial review.

Admissibility Basics

Not all evidence is admissible. Your attorney must establish that each piece of evidence is relevant to a contested issue, properly authenticated (proven to be what you claim it is), and not excluded by rules against hearsay, privilege, or other evidentiary barriers. Text messages must be attributed to a specific sender. Photographs must be verified for accuracy and timing. Financial documents must be connected to the person or account they purport to represent.

Evidence That Reliably Backfires

- Recordings made in violation of your state's consent laws—inadmissible and potentially criminal

- Evidence obtained by hacking into your spouse's phone, email, or accounts—inadmissible and can result in counter-claims

- Testimony from your children—judges resist placing children in the middle, and a parent who uses their child as a witness damages their own position

- Social media posts by your spouse that you screen-captured in a way that distorts context or timing

- Character witnesses who offer opinions but no firsthand observation of relevant facts

WHAT I'VE SEEN: The Recording That Destroyed Both Cases

Frank secretly recorded a phone conversation with his wife in which she admitted to hiding a bank account. Frank's state required two-party consent for recordings—meaning both parties must consent to being recorded. Frank's attorney attempted to introduce the recording at trial. The wife's attorney objected. The judge excluded the recording, sanctioned Frank for violating the wiretapping statute, and referred the matter for criminal investigation. The hidden bank account—which almost certainly would have produced sanctions against the wife had it been discovered through proper legal channels—was never addressed at trial because the only evidence of its existence was inadmissible. Frank's attempt at self-help destroyed the evidence trail that proper discovery would have preserved. Two wrongs. Zero justice.

Core Principle: *Evidence wins cases. Emotion loses them. Your documentation is the foundation on which every legal argument stands.*

CHAPTER 44

Documentation Strategies — Building Your Record from Day One

The moment you suspect divorce is possible—before you file, before you retain an attorney, before anything formal happens—begin building your documentary record. Every incident you log, every message you preserve, every financial statement you copy strengthens your position. Every gap in documentation is a gap your spouse's attorney will exploit.

✦ ✦ ✦

The Incident Log

A simple, contemporaneous record of significant events. For each entry: the date and time, a factual description of what occurred (observable behavior, not interpretation), the names of any witnesses, and any impact on the children. Keep the language clinical. 'On March 14 at 7:20 PM, the children reported they had not eaten dinner. Their father was asleep on the couch. I observed two empty beer bottles on the kitchen counter.' Not: 'He was drunk again and couldn't even feed the kids.' The first is evidence. The second is argument.

✦ ✦ ✦

Digital Evidence Capture

- Screenshot text messages with visible date and time stamps. Save the screenshots to cloud storage with automatic time-stamp preservation.

- Export entire text threads rather than individual messages—context matters, and opposing counsel will argue that cherry-picked messages distort the conversation.

- Save voicemails as audio files with the date and caller information preserved.

- Print social media posts with URLs, dates, and profile identification visible. Social media content can be deleted; your preserved copy cannot.

- Photograph physical evidence (property damage, injuries, unsafe conditions) with your phone's timestamp and location data enabled.

Financial Documentation

- Copy or photograph the last three to five years of joint tax returns

- Note current balances for every bank account, investment account, and retirement account you are aware of

- Save recent pay stubs, W-2s, and 1099s for both spouses

- Copy mortgage statements, car loan documents, and credit card statements

- Photograph or inventory valuable personal property: jewelry, art, collections, vehicles

Recording Laws

Thirty-eight states and the District of Columbia are one-party consent jurisdictions—you can record a conversation you are a participant in without the other person's knowledge. Twelve states require all-party consent—every participant must know and agree to the recording. Recording in violation of your state's law is a crime that can produce criminal liability, civil liability, and the exclusion of the recording from evidence.

Know your state's law before you record anything. Ask your attorney. This is not optional.

> **Core Principle:** *If you did not document it, it did not happen. Courts trust records. They distrust memory. Build your record as though every entry may be read aloud in a courtroom—because it might be.*

CHAPTER 45

Discovery — The Legal Tools That Uncover the Truth

Discovery is the most consequential phase of divorce litigation that most clients underestimate. It is the process through which each party compels the other to produce documents, answer questions under oath, and reveal information they might prefer to conceal. Discovery is where hidden assets surface, income fabrication collapses, and the factual foundation of the case is constructed.

The Discovery Tools

Interrogatories: Written questions that must be answered under oath within a specified time—typically thirty days. Questions target income sources, asset details, employment history, living arrangements, and any other facts relevant to the case.

Requests for production: Demands that the other party produce specific documents: bank statements, tax returns, business records, phone records, emails, text messages, insurance policies, loan applications, and any other records your attorney identifies as relevant.

Requests for admissions: Statements of fact that the other party must admit or deny under oath. Admissions narrow the disputed issues, and a fact admitted does not need to be proven at trial. A fact denied dishonestly becomes a credibility problem when the evidence contradicts the denial.

Depositions: Oral examination under oath, recorded by a court reporter. Your spouse answers questions from your attorney about finances, parenting, conduct, and any other relevant topic. Deposition testimony can be used at trial, and inconsistencies between deposition answers and trial testimony are devastating to credibility.

Subpoenas duces tecum: Court orders directing third parties— banks, employers, brokerage firms, phone companies—to produce records directly. Subpoenas bypass your spouse's control over what is disclosed and often reveal information your spouse failed to provide voluntarily.

Discovery Abuse and Judicial Sanctions

Spouses who obstruct discovery—producing incomplete records, claiming documents do not exist when they do, providing evasive answers to interrogatories, or destroying evidence—face escalating consequences:

- Court orders compelling production, with the obstructing party paying the cost of the motion
- Monetary sanctions for willful non-compliance
- Adverse inference: the court assumes that the concealed information is unfavorable to the concealing party
- Striking the non-compliant party's pleadings—effectively defaulting them on the contested issues
- Criminal contempt for flagrant refusal to comply with court-ordered production

WHAT I'VE SEEN: The Subpoena That Changed the Numbers

Georgia's husband Owen reported annual income of $110,000 on his financial disclosure. Georgia believed it was higher—Owen had purchased a new truck, taken the family on two overseas vacations, and renovated the kitchen during the year in question. Georgia's attorney issued subpoenas to Owen's employer, his bank, and three credit card companies. The employer records confirmed the base salary of $110,000 but revealed $48,000 in bonuses and $22,000 in stock vesting that Owen had not disclosed. The bank records showed $31,000 in deposits from a consulting side business Owen had never mentioned. The credit card statements revealed $14,000 in purchases from jewelry stores—gifts to a woman Georgia had not known about. Owen's actual income was $211,000—nearly double what he reported. The court imputed the full amount, sanctioned Owen for fraudulent disclosure, and awarded Georgia retroactive support based on the corrected figures. The subpoenas cost $1,800 to prepare and process. They produced a six-figure correction to the support calculation.

Core Principle: *Discovery is where the truth emerges or is buried. The effort you invest here determines whether your case rests on solid ground or on assumptions that opposing counsel will dismantle at trial.*

Field-tested tools for immediate use. Scripts enforce discipline under pressure. Templates structure documentation from day one.

PART XII

SCRIPTS, TEMPLATES, AND OPERATIONAL TOOLS

The three chapters that follow deliver practical instruments you can apply immediately. Communication scripts tested across thousands of cases. Sample courtroom Q&A modeled on testimony that wins. Evidence templates you can begin using tonight. Financial worksheets that organize the numbers your attorney needs to see. These are not theoretical frameworks—they are field-tested tools built for real-world stress.

CHAPTER 46

Communication Scripts for Every Stage of Divorce

When emotion clouds judgment, scripts provide clarity. The scripts below have been refined across decades of practice. Use them as written when your composure is compromised. Adapt them to your voice when you have the clarity to do so.

BIFF Scripts for Hostile Messages

Accusation About Parenting

Their message: "You're poisoning the kids against me. They don't even want to come to my house anymore."

Script: "The children will be ready for pickup at the scheduled time. If you have concerns about their transition, I'm willing to discuss them through our communication platform or with the therapist."

Financial Demand

Their message: "You owe me $500 for the kids' sports registration. Pay it today or I'm filing a motion."

Script: "I received your request regarding the sports registration. I'll review the expense against our agreement and respond within 48 hours."

Personal Attack

Their message: "Everyone knows what a fraud you are. My lawyer is going to expose you."

Script: No response required. Screenshot. Save. Log the date and time. Move on.

Scripts for Evaluators and Professionals

Opening Statement to a Custody Evaluator

Script: "Thank you for your time. I want to be as helpful and transparent as possible. I've brought documentation I thought might be useful, and I'm happy to answer any questions you have."

When Asked About Your Spouse's Weaknesses

Script: "[Spouse's name] has many qualities as a parent. My specific concern is [factual, behavioral description]. I can provide documentation that illustrates this pattern."

Scripts for Communicating with Your Attorney

Reporting a Development

Script: Subject line: "UPDATE — [Specific Issue]" Body: "On [date], the following occurred: [factual description]. Attached are [relevant documents/screenshots]. Please advise whether this warrants action."

Scripts for Your Children

When Your Child Asks Why

Script (ages 7–12): "We both love you so much. Sometimes adults decide they need to live in separate homes. This is a decision between us—not about you. Nothing you did caused this, and nothing you can do would change it. Both of us will always be your parents."

When Your Child Repeats the Other Parent's Negative Comments

Script: "I hear you. I'm sorry that was upsetting. You don't have to worry about grown-up problems. Your job is to be a kid, and both of your parents love you."

The Strategic Silence Protocol

Not every message requires a response. Before replying to any communication from your spouse, ask: Does this contain a logistical question that requires an answer? Does it involve the children's safety or schedule? If both answers are no, the strongest response is no response. Screenshot it. Log it. Walk away. Silence refuses engagement with the conflict cycle. It is not weakness. It is the most disciplined form of communication available to you.

> **Core Principle:** *These scripts work because they have been tested in thousands of cases. Use them when emotion clouds your judgment. Adapt them when you have clarity. Either way, let the script—not the anger—guide your fingers.*

CHAPTER 47

Evidence Templates, Financial Worksheets, and Case-Building Tools

What follows are the actual templates this book has described. They are formatted for immediate use. Print them. Photocopy them. Fill them in as events occur—not from memory weeks later. Contemporaneous records carry the weight of evidence. Reconstructed records carry the weight of argument.

Each template includes column headers, usage instructions, and enough space for multiple entries. Your attorney will recognize these formats. Judges will trust the organization they impose on your case.

TEMPLATE 1: INCIDENT LOG

USE FOR: *Parenting concerns, court order violations, substance abuse incidents, threatening or abusive behavior, unsafe conditions, any event you may need to reference in court.*

Instructions: Complete one row per incident. Write only observable facts—what you saw, heard, or were told by the children. Do not interpret or editorialize. 'Children reported they had not eaten dinner' is evidence. 'He neglected the children again' is argument.

Date	Time	What Happened (Observable Facts Only)	Witnesses Present	Impact on Children	Evidence Preserved

TEMPLATE 2: COMMUNICATION LOG

USE FOR: *Tracking all significant communications with your spouse, particularly hostile, manipulative, or threatening exchanges. Also useful for documenting communications with your spouse's attorney, evaluators, or other professionals.*

Instructions: Log every significant exchange. For texts and emails, note whether you preserved the original (screenshot, export, printout). For phone calls and in-person conversations, note the substance immediately after the conversation ends.

Date	Time	Channel	Who Initiated	Summary of Content	Your Response	Evidence Saved?

TEMPLATE 3: COURT ORDER VIOLATION TRACKER

USE FOR: *Building the pattern evidence required for contempt motions. Each entry should reference the specific paragraph of the court order violated. Patterns of violation are far more persuasive than isolated incidents.*

Instructions: Cite the specific order provision by paragraph number. Describe the violation factually. Attach or reference the evidence. Report every violation to your attorney promptly.

Date of Violation	Order Provision (Cite Paragraph #)	Nature of Violation (Factual Description)	Evidence (Describe/ Attach)	Reported to Attorney (Date)

TEMPLATE 4: PATTERN SUMMARY SHEET

USE FOR: *Connecting individual incidents into a credible narrative that demonstrates a sustained pattern of behavior. Courts respond to patterns. This template transforms your incident log entries into a persuasive summary.*

Instructions: Group related incidents by category (e.g., 'Late/Missed Pickups,' 'Substance Use During Parenting Time,' 'Financial Non-Compliance'). For each category, list the dates, brief descriptions, and the cumulative impact.

PATTERN CATEGORY: ____

Date	Incident (Brief Description)	Evidence Type (Log/Photo/Text/Record)	Impact on Children or Finances

CUMULATIVE IMPACT SUMMARY:

____

____

____

____

Duplicate this page for each pattern category. Common categories: Late/Missed Exchanges, Substance Use, Financial Non-Compliance, Communication Violations, Disparaging Remarks to Children, Failure to Follow Parenting Plan.

TEMPLATE 5: MONTHLY INCOME AND EXPENSE DECLARATION

USE FOR: *Establishing your monthly financial picture for support calculations, budgeting, and court filings. Most courts require a financial declaration—this template organizes the information your attorney needs to prepare it.*

SECTION A: MONTHLY INCOME

Income Source	Monthly Amount
Gross Wages / Salary	
Overtime	
Bonuses / Commissions (monthly average)	
Self-Employment Income (net)	
Rental Income (net)	
Investment Income (dividends, interest)	
Social Security / Disability	
Spousal Support Received	
Child Support Received	
Retirement / Pension Income	
Other Income (describe): _________________	
TOTAL MONTHLY GROSS INCOME	$ _____________

SECTION B: MONTHLY EXPENSES

Expense Category	Monthly Amount
HOUSING	
Mortgage / Rent	
Property Taxes	
Homeowner's / Renter's Insurance	
Utilities (electric, gas, water, sewer)	
Maintenance / Repairs	
HOA Fees	
TRANSPORTATION	
Car Payment	

Auto Insurance	
Fuel	
Maintenance / Repairs	
Registration / Tags	
FOOD	
Groceries	
Dining Out	
MEDICAL / HEALTH	
Health Insurance Premium (your share)	
Copays / Prescriptions	
Dental / Vision	
Therapy / Counseling	
CHILDREN	
School Tuition / Fees	
School Supplies / Uniforms	
Childcare / After-School	
Extracurricular Activities	
Clothing	
DEBT PAYMENTS	
Credit Card Minimum Payments	
Student Loans	
Personal Loans	
Other Debt: _________________	
PERSONAL	
Phone / Internet	
Personal Care / Grooming	
Clothing (yours)	
Subscriptions	
SAVINGS / RETIREMENT	
Retirement Contributions	
Emergency Savings	
OTHER	
_______________________	
_______________________	
TOTAL MONTHLY EXPENSES	$ __________
NET MONTHLY (Income – Expenses)	$ __________

TEMPLATE 6: MARITAL ASSET AND DEBT INVENTORY

USE FOR: *Creating a comprehensive inventory of every asset and debt for property division. Classification (Marital, Separate, or Disputed) determines what is divisible. Your attorney uses this to build the property division framework.*

Instructions: List every asset and debt you are aware of. Include approximate values. Mark classification based on your understanding—your attorney will confirm. Attach supporting documentation where available.

SECTION A: ASSETS

Asset Description	Approximate Current Value	Classification (M / S / D)	Title / Account Holder	Supporting Docs?

M = Marital | S = Separate | D = Disputed

✦ ✦ ✦

SECTION B: DEBTS

Debt Description	Current Balance	Monthly Payment	In Whose Name	Classification (M / S / D)	Supporting Docs?

TEMPLATE 7: HIDDEN ASSET RED FLAG CHECKLIST

USE FOR: *Identifying warning signs that your spouse may be concealing assets or underreporting income. If three or more flags are present, consult your attorney about engaging a forensic accountant.*

Indicator	YES	NO
Reported income is inconsistent with lifestyle (spending exceeds what income would support)		
New bank accounts, LLCs, trusts, or entities created in the past 24 months		
Large or unexplained cash withdrawals from joint accounts		
Overpayments to the IRS (creating a refund that arrives after divorce)		
Loans to friends, family members, or business associates		
Deferred bonuses, commissions, or contract payments		
Cryptocurrency purchases or digital wallet activity		
Salary or bonus paid to a new romantic partner through a business		
Resistance or delay in producing financial documents during discovery		
Sudden decrease in reported business revenue or income		
Unexplained transfers to unfamiliar accounts or individuals		
Purchases of easily concealed valuables (art, jewelry, collectibles, precious metals)		
Post office box or mail diverted to a separate address		
Recent changes to passwords on financial accounts		

TOTAL "YES" RESPONSES: _______ / 14

3 or more: Consult your attorney about engaging a forensic accountant.

5 or more: Forensic investigation should be considered a priority, not an option.

TEMPLATE 8: ALIMONY FACTOR SUMMARY SHEET

USE FOR: *Organizing the factors courts consider when determining spousal support. Complete this with your attorney to assess strength on each factor.*

Factor	Your Position (Strong / Neutral / Weak)	Notes / Evidence
Length of marriage		
Income disparity between spouses		
Standard of living during marriage		
Age and health of both parties		
Earning capacity of requesting spouse		
Time out of workforce		
Education / training needed		
Contributions to spouse's career or education		
Childcare responsibilities affecting employment		
Marital misconduct (if applicable in jurisdiction)		
Available assets after property division		
Tax consequences of proposed arrangement		

TEMPLATE 9: PRE-MEDIATION PREPARATION WORKSHEET

USE FOR: *Completing before every mediation session. Mediators report that prepared participants reach better agreements faster and at lower cost.*

Preparation Item	Your Answer
My 3 highest priorities in order	
My walk-away point (minimum I will accept)	
What I am willing to concede	
Current financial figures I must know (income, accounts, property values)	
Proposed parenting schedule (with 2–3 alternatives)	
What would a judge likely order if mediation fails?	
Supporting documents I am bringing	
Issues I expect the other side to raise	
My emotional triggers and how I will manage them	

TEMPLATE 10: PRE-TRIAL PREPARATION CHECKLIST

USE FOR: *The week before any hearing or trial. Review with your attorney. Check each item as completed.*

☐	Task
☐	Met with attorney to review testimony outline and key exhibits
☐	Reviewed every document that may be referenced during testimony
☐	Practiced answering anticipated cross-examination questions aloud
☐	Prepared evidence binder with tabbed exhibits organized by issue
☐	Selected conservative, professional attire (laid out the night before)
☐	Confirmed courtroom location, parking, and arrival time
☐	Arranged childcare — children should NEVER attend divorce hearings
☐	Prepared: photo ID, pen, notepad, water, any medications needed
☐	Phone fully charged, then set to SILENT before entering courthouse
☐	Confirmed arrival time: at least 30 minutes early
☐	Reviewed the 'Language That Strengthens vs. Destroys' guide (Chapter 36)
☐	Identified the 3 strongest points in my case and can state each in under 30 seconds
☐	Identified the 2 weakest points and have honest, composed responses prepared
☐	Eaten a full meal — low blood sugar impairs composure and clarity

TEMPLATE 11: WITNESS LIST AND CONTACT SHEET

USE FOR: *Identifying and organizing every potential witness. Your attorney uses this to evaluate who strengthens the case and who may create risk.*

Witness Name	Relationship to Case	Phone / Email	What They Can Testify To	Strength (1–5)	Risks / Limitations

TEMPLATE 12: EVIDENCE INDEX AND BINDER ORGANIZATION GUIDE

USE FOR: *Creating the master index for your evidence binder. Organize exhibits by category. Tab each section. Number each exhibit sequentially. This is the document your attorney will use to locate evidence during hearings and trial.*

Exhibit #	Description	Category (Financial / Custody / Communication / Other)	Date of Document	Binder Tab #	Authenticated?

Suggested binder tab categories: (1) Financial Records, (2) Income/Employment, (3) Parenting Documentation, (4) Communications, (5) Photographs/Video, (6) Professional Reports, (7) Court Orders, (8) Miscellaneous.

TEMPLATE 13: LAWYER CONSULTATION INTERVIEW SCORECARD

USE FOR: *Evaluating attorneys during initial consultations. Complete one scorecard per attorney. Compare scores before making your hiring decision.*

Attorney Name: _______________________________ Date: _____________

Referred by: ____

Evaluation Criteria	Score (1–5)	Notes
Years practicing family law exclusively		
Number of cases taken to trial		
Described a clear strategy for my type of case		
Communication protocol (response time, update schedule)		
Identified who will handle my case day-to-day		
Explained fee structure clearly and provided cost range		
Listened more than talked during the consultation		
Focused on strategy rather than promising aggression		
Appeared knowledgeable about issues specific to my case		
I felt heard, respected, and taken seriously		
TOTAL SCORE	_______ / 50	

Retainer quoted: $ _________________ Hourly rate: $ _______________

Overall gut feeling (1–10): _________

Would I trust this person in a courtroom representing my family? YES / NO

> **Core Principle:** *These templates work because they impose structure on chaos. Use them from day one. Update them consistently. Bring them to every attorney meeting. They transform scattered observations into organized evidence—the raw material from which your case is built.*

CHAPTER 48

Sample Courtroom Q&A for Divorce Testimony

What follows are sample question-and-answer exchanges modeled on the testimony patterns I have seen produce the strongest results across decades of trial practice. Study these before you take the stand. Read the answers aloud. Notice their length—short, specific, grounded in facts rather than emotion. Practice answering in this style until it becomes reflexive.

Direct Examination: Property Division

Q: *Can you describe the major assets of the marriage?*

A: Yes. The marital home at 412 Oakwood Drive, which was appraised at $385,000 with a mortgage balance of approximately $242,000. A joint savings account at First National with a current balance of $31,400. My 401(k) through my employer, with a marital portion of approximately $218,000. My wife's IRA with a balance of approximately $67,000. Two vehicles, a 2021 Honda CR-V and a 2019 Ford F-150. And household furnishings.

Q: *How do you know these figures?*

A: I reviewed the most recent statements for each account, which are included in the exhibits. The home appraisal was conducted by a licensed appraiser on September 14 of this year.

Q: *Are you aware of any assets your spouse has not disclosed?*

A: I believe there are. During our marriage, my spouse opened a brokerage account at Charles Schwab that does not appear on the financial disclosure. I became aware of it through a statement that arrived at the house in January of this year. I preserved that statement and provided it to my attorney.

◆ ◆ ◆

Direct Examination: Spousal Support

Q: *What is your current employment situation?*

A: I am working part-time as an administrative assistant, earning $24,000 per year. Prior to our marriage, I was employed as a marketing coordinator earning approximately $52,000. I left that position in 2014 when our first child was born, at my husband's request.

Q: *What steps have you taken to increase your earning capacity?*

A: I enrolled in a digital marketing certificate program at the community college in August. I expect to complete it in May. I have also updated my resume and met with a career counselor through the college's placement office. My goal is to return to marketing within twelve months of completing the program.

Q: *Why can't you return to your prior salary immediately?*

A: The marketing field has changed significantly in the ten years since I left. The tools, platforms, and certifications that employers require today did not exist when I was working. The certificate program addresses that gap, but I cannot erase a decade of absence overnight.

Cross-Examination Defense: Attacks on Financial Credibility

Q: *Isn't it true you withdrew $8,000 from the joint account last March without telling your husband?*

A: I withdrew $8,000 in March to retain an attorney. I did not notify him in advance because I was concerned about his reaction based on prior incidents. The withdrawal is documented in the bank records and was disclosed in my financial declaration.

Q: *So you took money from the marriage without permission?*

A: I used marital funds to retain legal counsel, which I was entitled to do. The amount was reasonable for a retainer, and it was fully disclosed.

Cross-Examination Defense: Attacks on Parenting

Q: *Your daughter has missed six days of school this semester. You were the parent responsible on each of those mornings. Is that correct?*

A: She missed four days due to illness—I have the pediatrician's notes for each absence. She missed one day for a pre-scheduled dental procedure. The sixth absence occurred on a day when my car would not start, and I called the school to report the absence within thirty minutes. I do not have a pattern of school absences during my parenting time.

Q: *You don't think six absences is a problem?*

A: I think four sick days, one dental visit, and one car breakdown over five months is a normal range for any parent. I take my daughter's attendance seriously and I have the records to show it.

Cross-Examination Defense: Substance Abuse Allegations

Q: *Isn't it true that you have a history of alcohol abuse?*

A: I developed a problem with alcohol three years ago. I recognized it, entered treatment voluntarily, and have been sober for twenty-six months. I attend AA weekly, I see my counselor monthly, and I have submitted to every drug and alcohol test ordered by this court. All results have been negative.

Q: *How can the court be confident you won't relapse?*

A: I cannot guarantee the future. What I can demonstrate is twenty-six months of sustained sobriety, consistent treatment, and a support network that I rely on daily. I take this seriously because my children depend on me.

The Recovery Technique

If you misspeak on the stand or realize you gave an incomplete or inaccurate answer, correct it at the earliest opportunity—either during redirect or by asking the judge's permission to clarify. "Your Honor, I would like to correct something I said earlier. When I was asked about the March withdrawal, I stated the amount was $8,000. Having reviewed the statement during the break, the actual amount was $7,500. I want the record to be accurate."

Self-correction demonstrates honesty. Allowing an error to stand and having it exposed by opposing counsel demonstrates either dishonesty or carelessness. Neither serves you.

> **Core Principle:** *Practice these scenarios before you take the stand. Familiarity breeds composure. Composure breeds believability. And believability determines the outcome.*

CHAPTER 49

Life After Judgment: The Long Game

The judge signs the decree. The case number closes. Your attorney sends a final bill. And then you walk out of the courthouse into a life that no longer has a docket number attached to it.

Most divorce books end at the judgment. This one does not. Because the decisions you make in the months and years after your decree will determine whether the outcome you fought for actually holds—or erodes through neglect, provocation, or the slow drift of unfinished emotional business.

Enforcement Is Not Optional

A decree that is not enforced is a suggestion. If your former spouse violates the parenting schedule, fails to pay support, ignores the re-financing deadline, or disregards any other provision, you have two choices: enforce or accept. There is no third option.

Enforcement does not require hostility. It requires documentation and discipline—the same two pillars that won your case. Log every violation using the Court Order Violation Tracker from Chapter 47. Report each one to your attorney. When the pattern is sufficient, file a contempt motion. Courts take enforcement seriously when you present a documented pattern rather than a single frustrated complaint.

The clients who lose ground after judgment are not the ones with weak decrees. They are the ones who stop documenting, stop enforcing, and allow small violations to accumulate into a new status quo that their former spouse then argues the court should ratify.

◆ ◆ ◆

Financial Reconstruction

Divorce is a financial earthquake. Even in the best outcomes, your household income is now supporting two homes instead of one. Reconstruction begins immediately.

The first 90 days:

Establish a post-divorce budget based on your actual new income and expenses—not what you hope they will be. Use the Monthly Income and Expense Declaration from Chapter 47 as your framework. Open individual accounts if you have not already. Close or remove your name from joint accounts as directed by the decree. Update every beneficiary designation: life insurance, retirement accounts, bank accounts, transfer-on-death deeds. Update your will, power of attorney, and healthcare directive. These documents still name your former spouse unless you change them.

The first year:

Meet with a financial advisor—ideally a Certified Divorce Financial Analyst or a fee-only planner—to recalibrate your retirement projections, investment strategy, and tax planning. If you received a QDRO, confirm it has been submitted to the plan administrator and that the transfer is complete. If the decree requires your former spouse to refinance the marital home, monitor the deadline. If the deadline passes without action, enforce.

The long view:

Rebuild your credit independently. Apply for a credit card in your own name if you do not have one. Pay it in full each month. Your credit history during the marriage may have been entirely in your spouse's name, and you are effectively starting over. This is not failure. It is the normal consequence of separating intertwined financial lives.

✦ ✦ ✦

Co-Parenting Beyond the Courthouse

The parenting plan is a floor, not a ceiling. The minimum requirements for co-parenting are spelled out in your decree. What happens above that minimum is determined by the two of you—and, over time, by your children's evolving needs.

The clients who co-parent most effectively after judgment share three characteristics. They communicate through the platform, not around it. They respond to logistics and ignore provocations. And they make decisions based on what their children need today, not on what their spouse did during the marriage.

Your children will grow. Schedules that worked for a six-year-old will not work for a fourteen-year-old. Extracurricular activities, friendships, and eventually driving will reshape the logistics. The parents who handle these transitions well are the ones who built flexibility into their plan and maintained enough discipline in their communication to negotiate adjustments without returning to court.

If your former spouse remains high-conflict, maintain parallel parenting. Do not attempt collaboration with someone who weaponizes every interaction. Protect the boundaries. Use the platform. Let your attorney handle anything that exceeds the plan's dispute resolution mechanism.

New Relationships

You will eventually want to date. When you do, the discipline that protected your case must now protect your children.

Do not introduce a new partner to your children until the relationship is stable—six months at minimum, longer if your children are still adjusting. Do not allow a new partner to assume a parenting role. Do not post about your new relationship on social media in ways that your former spouse or your children will encounter. And do not allow a new partner to be present during exchanges or to communicate with your former spouse.

The clients who damage their post-judgment stability most severely are the ones who move a new partner into the home within months of the decree, force introductions before the children are ready, and create exactly the instability that the court ordered them to avoid.

Emotional Recovery

Litigation is trauma. Even when you win, the process leaves marks—hypervigilance, difficulty trusting, anger that surfaces without warning, exhaustion that sleep does not cure. These are normal responses to an abnormal experience.

Therapy is not a sign of weakness. It is the most efficient tool available for processing what happened, separating your identity from the case, and rebuilding the emotional capacity that sustained conflict depletes. If you were in therapy during the divorce, continue. If you were not, start now. The post-judgment period is when the adrenaline fades and the full weight of the experience lands.

Your children are processing their own version of this experience. Watch for changes in sleep, appetite, school performance, social withdrawal, or behavioral regression. These are signals, not problems. Respond with stability, consistency, and professional support when needed. Do not ask your children to process your emotions. That is your therapist's role, not theirs.

The Five-Year View

Five years from now, the details of the litigation will have faded. The motions, the hearings, the temporary orders, the depositions—they will blur into a difficult chapter rather than a defining one. What will remain is the life you built after the decree was signed.

The clients I hear from years later—the ones who are doing well— share a common thread. They stopped litigating their marriage and started building their future. They enforced their decree when necessary but did not use enforcement as a weapon. They put their children's stability ahead of their own anger. They rebuilt their finances with patience rather than panic. And they allowed themselves to heal at a pace that respected the magnitude of what they had been through.

The ones who are not doing well are still fighting. Still documenting every perceived slight. Still using the children as messengers, witnesses, or allies. Still defining themselves by what their former spouse did rather than by what they are building.

You have a choice. The decree is signed. The case is closed. The system you learned in this book—the Four Pillars of Stability, Credibility,

Documentation, and Discipline—does not expire when the judge signs the order. It is the framework for the life that comes next.

> **Core Principle:** *The goal was never court. The goal was always a durable life. You now have the tools to build one.*

Quick-Reference Divorce Checklists

Checklist 1: Before Filing for Divorce

- ☐ Secure copies of the last 3–5 years of joint tax returns
- ☐ Photograph or copy recent statements for all bank, investment, and retirement accounts
- ☐ Note current balances and account numbers for every financial account
- ☐ Copy recent pay stubs, W-2s, and 1099s for both spouses
- ☐ Copy mortgage statements, vehicle loan documents, and credit card statements
- ☐ Photograph or inventory valuable personal property (jewelry, art, collections)
- ☐ Secure important personal documents: birth certificates, passports, Social Security cards
- ☐ Establish an individual bank account if you do not have one
- ☐ Identify 3–5 family law attorneys and schedule consultations
- ☐ Begin a private incident log if concerning behavior is present
- ☐ Review and understand your household monthly expenses
- ☐ Assess your credit by obtaining a free credit report

✦ ✦ ✦

Checklist 2: Financial Document Collection

- ☐ Joint and individual tax returns (3–5 years)
- ☐ W-2s, 1099s, and K-1s for both spouses
- ☐ Pay stubs (3 months minimum)
- ☐ Bank statements: all joint and individual accounts (12 months)
- ☐ Investment and brokerage account statements (12 months)
- ☐ Retirement account statements: 401(k), IRA, pension (most recent)
- ☐ Mortgage statements and property tax records
- ☐ Vehicle titles, loan statements, and registration
- ☐ Credit card statements (12 months)
- ☐ Business tax returns and financial statements (if applicable)
- ☐ Insurance policies: life, health, auto, homeowners
- ☐ Estate planning documents: wills, trusts, powers of attorney
- ☐ Loan applications submitted during the marriage (contain asset/income declarations)
- ☐ Prenuptial or postnuptial agreements

◆ ◆ ◆

Checklist 3: Before Mediation

- ☐ Define your three highest priorities
- ☐ Identify your walk-away points (minimum acceptable outcomes)
- ☐ Know current account balances, property values, and income figures
- ☐ Prepare a written monthly expense worksheet
- ☐ Bring proposed parenting schedule(s) with 2–3 alternatives

- ☐ Review your attorney's assessment of likely court outcomes
- ☐ Bring supporting documents for every contested issue
- ☐ Eat a full meal and bring water—sessions can last hours
- ☐ Leave your phone on silent and resist checking it during breaks

✦ ✦ ✦

Checklist 4: Before a Hearing or Trial

- ☐ Meet with your attorney to review testimony outline and key exhibits
- ☐ Review every document that may be referenced during your testimony
- ☐ Practice answering anticipated cross-examination questions aloud
- ☐ Prepare a binder with tabbed exhibits organized by issue
- ☐ Select conservative, professional attire
- ☐ Confirm the courtroom location, parking, and arrival time
- ☐ Arrange childcare—children should never attend divorce hearings
- ☐ Bring photo ID, a pen, a notepad, and water
- ☐ Silence your phone completely before entering the courthouse
- ☐ Arrive at least 30 minutes early

✦ ✦ ✦

Checklist 5: Before a Deposition

- ☐ Meet with your attorney for deposition preparation
- ☐ Review all documents you have produced in discovery

- ☐ Practice the pause: wait 2–3 seconds before answering every question
- ☐ Understand the rules: answer only the question asked, do not volunteer
- ☐ Know how to say "I don't recall" without appearing evasive
- ☐ Dress professionally—the deposition is recorded and may be shown to the judge
- ☐ Bring nothing you are not prepared to produce—opposing counsel may request anything in your possession

✦ ✦ ✦

Checklist 6: After Final Judgment

- ☐ Read the entire decree and confirm you understand every provision
- ☐ Confirm QDRO has been prepared and filed for retirement account division
- ☐ Monitor refinancing deadline for the marital home
- ☐ Update beneficiaries on life insurance, retirement accounts, and bank accounts
- ☐ Update your will, power of attorney, and healthcare directive
- ☐ Close or remove your name from joint accounts as directed by the decree
- ☐ Update your name on driver's license, Social Security, and other documents if applicable
- ☐ Establish a post-divorce budget
- ☐ Meet with a financial advisor to recalibrate retirement planning
- ☐ Continue or begin therapy for emotional processing

✦ ✦ ✦

Checklist 7: Emergency and Safety Protocol

- ☐ If in immediate danger, call 911
- ☐ National Domestic Violence Hotline: 1-800-799-7233 (SAFE)
- ☐ Develop a safety plan with a DV advocate or counselor
- ☐ Identify a safe location (friend, family, shelter) for you and the children
- ☐ Pack an emergency bag: ID, keys, phone/charger, medication, cash, children's essentials
- ☐ Secure copies of critical documents in a location your spouse cannot access
- ☐ File for a protective order at the nearest courthouse or through your attorney
- ☐ Document all incidents: photographs, dates, descriptions, witnesses
- ☐ Change passwords on personal accounts, email, and financial platforms
- ☐ If children are present, contact your attorney about emergency custody provisions

Sample Settlement Agreement Clauses

The clauses below are illustrative models—not jurisdiction-specific legal forms. They demonstrate the level of specificity that prevents future litigation. Every clause in your agreement should be reviewed by your attorney before signing.

✦ ✦ ✦

Property Division

"The marital residence located at [address] shall be listed for sale within sixty (60) days of the entry of this decree. Both parties shall cooperate in selecting a real estate agent and setting the listing price at fair market value. Net proceeds, after payment of the mortgage balance, closing costs, and any agreed repairs, shall be divided equally (50/50) between the parties."

"Husband shall retain the 2021 Honda CR-V. Wife shall retain the 2019 Toyota Camry. Each party assumes any outstanding loan balance on their respective vehicle and shall hold the other harmless from any liability thereon."

✦ ✦ ✦

Spousal Support

"Husband shall pay Wife rehabilitative spousal support of $3,500 per month, commencing on the first day of the month following entry of this decree, and continuing for a period of forty-eight (48) months. Support shall terminate automatically upon the earlier of: (a) the expiration of the forty-eight-month period; (b) the death of either party; (c) the remarriage of Wife; (d) the cohabitation of Wife with an unrelated adult in a conjugal relationship for a period exceeding ninety (90) consecutive days."

Child Support — Incidental Expenses

"In addition to the base child support obligation, the parties shall share equally (50/50) the following incidental expenses: (a) unreimbursed medical, dental, and vision expenses exceeding $250 per child per calendar year; (b) agreed-upon extracurricular activities; (c) school-related expenses including tuition, uniforms, and required supplies. Neither party shall enroll a child in any activity or program costing more than $500 per season without the prior written consent of the other party."

Communication Protocol

"All non-emergency communication between the parties regarding the minor children shall be conducted exclusively through the OurFamilyWizard platform. Neither party shall communicate through personal text message, social media, or third parties regarding parenting matters. Emergency communications (defined as situations involving imminent risk to a child's health or safety) may be made by telephone."

Social Media and Privacy

"Neither party shall post photographs, videos, or identifying information about the minor children on any social media platform without the prior written consent of the other party. Neither party shall make disparaging statements about the other party on social media or in the presence of the minor children."

Relocation Restriction

"Neither party shall relocate with the minor children more than fifty (50) miles from the current primary residence without either: (a) the written consent of the other party; or (b) an order of the court following a hearing on the matter. The relocating party shall provide written notice of intent to relocate at least ninety (90) days prior to the proposed move."

Dispute Resolution

"Before filing any post-judgment motion with the court (other than an emergency motion), the parties shall first attempt to resolve the dispute through mediation with a mutually agreed-upon mediator. The cost of mediation shall be shared equally. If mediation does not resolve the dispute within thirty (30) days, either party may then file an appropriate motion with the court."

Life Insurance Provision

"Husband shall maintain a life insurance policy with a death benefit of not less than $500,000 naming Wife as irrevocable beneficiary for so long as the spousal support obligation remains in effect. Husband shall provide proof of coverage to Wife annually on or before January 15 of each year."

✦ ✦ ✦

New Partner — Overnight Introduction

"Neither party shall introduce a new romantic partner to the minor children until that relationship has been established for a minimum of six (6) months and the other parent has been provided with thirty (30) days' advance written notice. Neither party shall allow a romantic partner who is not a spouse to be present in the home overnight during the children's parenting time for the first twelve (12) months following the entry of this decree."

> **Core Principle:** *These clauses demonstrate what specificity looks like in practice. Vague agreements breed litigation. Precise agreements prevent it. Invest the drafting time now to avoid the courtroom later.*

APPENDIX C

Glossary of Divorce and Family Law Terms

The terms below appear throughout this book and in courtrooms, mediation sessions, and attorney offices across the country. Understanding them gives you command of the language your case will be conducted in.

A

Adjudication. A final decision or judgment by a court on the contested issues in a case.

Admissible Evidence. Evidence that meets the legal standards for consideration by the court, including relevance and proper authentication.

Affidavit. A written statement of facts made under oath and signed before a notary or other authorized official.

Alimony. Financial support paid by one spouse to the other after divorce. Also called spousal support or maintenance.

Alternative Dispute Resolution (ADR). Methods of resolving disputes outside of trial, including mediation, arbitration, and collaborative divorce.

286

Annulment. A legal proceeding that declares a marriage void, as though it never legally existed.

Answer. The formal written response filed by the respondent to the petitioner's divorce complaint.

Appeal. A request to a higher court to review and reverse or modify a lower court's decision.

Appraisal. A professional assessment of the fair market value of property, typically real estate.

Arbitration. A dispute resolution process where a neutral arbitrator hears evidence and issues a decision, which may be binding or non-binding.

Arrearage. Unpaid amounts owed under a court order, typically for child support or spousal support.

Asset. Anything of value owned by either spouse, including real property, bank accounts, investments, retirement funds, vehicles, and personal property.

Automatic Temporary Restraining Order (ATRO). Court orders that automatically take effect upon filing for divorce, prohibiting both parties from dissipating assets, canceling insurance, or hiding property.

B

BAH (Basic Allowance for Housing). A military housing stipend that may be included in income calculations for support purposes.

Best Interests of the Child. The legal standard courts apply when making custody and visitation decisions, considering the child's safety, stability, and well-being.

BIFF Method. A communication framework (Brief, Informative, Friendly, Firm) for managing exchanges with a difficult co-parent.

Burden of Proof. The obligation to prove contested facts, typically resting on the party making the allegation.

C

CDFA (Certified Divorce Financial Analyst). A financial professional who models the long-term economic impact of proposed divorce settlements.

Child Support. Court-ordered payments from one parent to the other for the financial support of minor children.

Child Support Guidelines. State-specific formulas used to calculate the presumptive child support obligation based on parental income and custody arrangement.

Coercive Control. A sustained pattern of psychological domination through monitoring, isolation, restriction, and fear, increasingly recognized as domestic violence.

Collaborative Divorce. A process in which both spouses and their attorneys commit to resolving the case without court intervention, with a disqualification provision if the process fails.

Commingling. Mixing separate property with marital property in a way that makes the separate property difficult or impossible to identify.

Community Property. A property division system used in approximately nine states where assets acquired during the marriage are owned equally by both spouses.

Complaint (Petition). The initial legal document filed to begin a divorce proceeding, also called a petition for dissolution.

Contempt of Court. Willful violation of a court order, punishable by fines, sanctions, or imprisonment.

Contested Divorce. A divorce in which the spouses cannot agree on one or more issues, requiring judicial resolution.

Coparenting. The shared responsibility of raising children after separation or divorce.

Coparenting Platform. Digital applications (OurFamilyWizard, TalkingParents, AppClose) that create unalterable records of parental communications.

Coverture Fraction. The formula used to calculate the marital portion of a pension: years of service during the marriage divided by total years of service.

Cross-Examination. Questioning of a witness by the opposing party's attorney, intended to challenge credibility and test the accuracy of testimony.

Custody Evaluation. A comprehensive assessment of the family by a mental health professional, resulting in recommendations to the court regarding custody and parenting time.

D

DARVO. A manipulation pattern: Deny, Attack, Reverse Victim and Offender. Common in high-conflict personalities.

Date of Separation. The date on which the marital partnership effectively ended, significant for property classification and valuation.

Date of Valuation. The specific date on which marital assets are valued for purposes of division; varies by jurisdiction.

Decree (Final Judgment). The court's final order dissolving the marriage and establishing the rights and obligations of both parties.

Default Judgment. A judgment entered when one party fails to respond to the divorce filing within the required time.

Deferred Compensation. Employment benefits payable at a future date, such as stock options, RSUs, or executive retirement plans.

Deposition. Sworn oral testimony taken outside the courtroom, recorded by a court reporter, used in preparation for trial.

Direct Examination. Questioning of a witness by the attorney who called that witness, intended to present the witness's narrative.

Discovery. The legal process through which each party compels the other to disclose documents, answer questions, and produce evidence.

Dissipation. The waste or destruction of marital assets by one spouse for a purpose unrelated to the marriage during the period of breakdown.

Domestic Violence. Physical, emotional, psychological, sexual, financial, or digital abuse committed by one intimate partner against the other.

E

Emancipation. The legal point at which a child is no longer considered a minor, typically at age eighteen, ending the child support obligation.

Emergency Protective Order (EPO). A short-term protective order issued by law enforcement at the scene of a domestic violence incident.

Equitable Distribution. A property division system used by the majority of states where marital property is divided fairly, though not necessarily equally.

EtG Testing. Ethyl glucuronide testing that detects alcohol metabolites for approximately eighty hours after consumption.

Evidence Binder. An organized collection of documents, photographs, and records assembled for presentation at hearings or trial.

Ex Parte. A court proceeding or order made at the request of one party without the other party present, typically in emergency situations.

Expert Witness. A professional with specialized knowledge who provides testimony to help the court understand complex issues.

F

Fault Divorce. A divorce granted on specific grounds such as adultery, cruelty, abandonment, or substance abuse, as opposed to no-fault dissolution.

Filing Status. The tax classification (married filing jointly, married filing separately, head of household, single) that applies for the tax year in which the divorce occurs.

Forensic Accountant. A financial investigator who traces assets, reconstructs income, analyzes business valuations, and identifies hidden or underreported wealth.

G

GAL (Guardian ad Litem). An attorney or qualified professional appointed by the court to represent the best interests of the child in custody proceedings.

Goodwill. The intangible value of a business beyond its physical assets, including reputation, client relationships, and earning capacity.

Gray Rock Method. A communication strategy of being emotionally unreactive and uninteresting to a high-conflict personality.

H

Hearing. A court proceeding where evidence and arguments are presented on a specific issue, shorter than a full trial.

Hearsay. An out-of-court statement offered for the truth of its content, generally inadmissible unless an exception applies.

I

Imputed Income. Income attributed to a spouse by the court based on earning capacity when actual income appears artificially reduced.

Incident Log. A contemporaneous record of significant events, maintained with dates, facts, and witnesses.

Interrogatories. Written questions served on the opposing party that must be answered under oath within a specified timeframe.

J

Joint Legal Custody. A custody arrangement in which both parents share decision-making authority regarding the child's education, healthcare, and religion.

Joint Physical Custody. A custody arrangement in which the child spends significant time living with both parents.

Jurisdiction. The authority of a specific court to hear and decide a case, determined by geographic location and subject matter.

L

Legal Separation. A court order that establishes rights and obligations between spouses who remain legally married but live apart.

Limited-Scope Representation. Hiring an attorney for specific tasks rather than full case representation, also called unbundled legal services.

Lump-Sum Alimony. A single payment or fixed series of payments totaling a defined amount, providing finality to the support obligation.

M

Marital Property. Assets and debts acquired during the marriage through the efforts, labor, or expenditure of either spouse.

Material Change in Circumstances. The legal threshold required for modifying existing court orders regarding custody, support, or other provisions.

Mediation. A dispute resolution process in which a neutral mediator facilitates negotiation between the parties.

Modification. A court-approved change to an existing order, typically for custody, support, or parenting time.

Morality Clause. A provision in a parenting plan restricting overnight romantic guests during the children's parenting time.

Motion. A formal written request to the court for a specific ruling or order.

Motion to Compel. A request asking the court to force the opposing party to comply with discovery obligations.

N

Narcissistic Pattern. A personality pattern characterized by extreme self-focus, impression management, inability to empathize, and viewing the divorce as a competition to be won.

No-Fault Divorce. A divorce granted without requiring proof of wrongdoing by either spouse, based on irreconcilable differences or irretrievable breakdown.

Noncustodial Parent. The parent with whom the child does not primarily reside.

O

Order of Protection. A court order prohibiting contact, requiring distance, and potentially granting temporary custody and exclusive possession of the residence to the protected party.

P

Parallel Parenting. A co-parenting model in which each parent operates independently during their parenting time, minimizing direct interaction.

Parental Alienation. A campaign by one parent to undermine, damage, or destroy the child's relationship with the other parent.

Parenting Coordinator. A neutral professional appointed to resolve day-to-day co-parenting disputes without returning to court.

Parenting Plan. A written agreement specifying the custody schedule, decision-making responsibilities, communication protocols, and dispute resolution mechanisms.

Pendente Lite. Latin for "pending the litigation." Temporary orders that remain in effect until the final decree.

Pension. A retirement benefit that pays a monthly income based on years of service and salary, divisible in divorce using the coverture fraction.

Perjury. The crime of making false statements under oath.

Permanent Alimony. Spousal support with no defined end date, typically reserved for long marriages with significant income disparity.

Petition (Complaint). The initial document filed to commence divorce proceedings.

Petitioner. The spouse who files for divorce, also called the plaintiff.

Prenuptial Agreement. A contract between prospective spouses governing property rights and support obligations in the event of divorce.

Pro Se. Representing yourself in court without an attorney. Also called self-representation.

Q

QDRO (Qualified Domestic Relations Order). A court order directing a retirement plan administrator to divide retirement benefits between the spouses.

R

Rehabilitative Alimony. Spousal support for a defined period to allow the recipient to obtain education, training, or employment.

Reimbursement Alimony. Support awarded to compensate one spouse for specific financial sacrifices made to support the other's education or career.

Request for Admissions. A discovery tool requiring the opposing party to admit or deny specific factual statements under oath.

Request for Production. A discovery demand requiring the opposing party to produce specified documents and records.

Respondent. The spouse who receives the divorce filing and must respond, also called the defendant.

Retainer. An upfront deposit paid to an attorney, drawn against as legal work is performed.

S

SCRA (Servicemembers Civil Relief Act). Federal law protecting active-duty military members from default judgments and providing stays of proceedings during deployment.

SCRAM Monitor. Secure Continuous Remote Alcohol Monitor—an ankle bracelet providing twenty-four-hour transdermal alcohol detection.

Separate Property. Assets owned by one spouse before the marriage, gifts received individually, or inheritances, which are generally not divisible.

Settlement Agreement. A written contract between divorcing spouses resolving all contested issues, submitted to the court for approval.

Soberlink. A portable breathalyzer with facial recognition and GPS that transmits real-time results to the court and attorneys.

Sole Legal Custody. A custody arrangement in which one parent has exclusive authority to make major decisions regarding the child.

Status Quo. The existing arrangement—particularly regarding custody—that courts are reluctant to disrupt absent compelling reason.

Step-Down Schedule. An alimony structure in which the monthly payment decreases at defined intervals over time.

Stipulation. An agreement between the parties on a specific issue, submitted to the court and made part of the order.

Subpoena. A court order compelling a person to appear and testify or produce documents.

Subpoena Duces Tecum. A subpoena requiring production of specific documents or records from a third party.

Supervised Visitation. Parenting time that occurs in the presence of a court-approved supervisor, ordered when safety concerns exist.

T

Temporary Orders. Court orders governing custody, support, and property matters while the divorce is pending.

Testimony. Statements made under oath by a witness during a hearing or trial.

Transmutation. The legal process by which separate property becomes marital property through commingling, retitling, or joint use.

Trial. A formal court proceeding where evidence is presented, witnesses testify, and the judge issues a final ruling.

TRO (Temporary Restraining Order). A short-term court order issued on an emergency basis, typically lasting until a full hearing can be held.

U

UCCJEA (Uniform Child Custody Jurisdiction and Enforcement Act). A law adopted in all fifty states determining which state has jurisdiction over custody matters.

Uncontested Divorce. A divorce in which both parties agree on all terms, requiring no judicial resolution of disputed issues.

USFSPA (Uniformed Services Former Spouses' Protection Act). Federal law authorizing state courts to divide military retirement pay in divorce.

V

Vocational Evaluation. A professional assessment of a spouse's earning capacity based on education, skills, work history, and the labor market.

W

Wage Garnishment. A court-ordered deduction from a person's wages to satisfy a support or debt obligation.

APPENDIX D

Additional Resources and Support

The resources listed below are current as of the publication date. Websites, phone numbers, and organizational structures change. Verify availability before relying on any specific resource.

Legal Resources

- American Bar Association Family Law Section: americanbar.org/groups/family_law

- State Bar Lawyer Referral Services: contact your state bar association for a directory of family law attorneys accepting referrals

- Legal Services Corporation (legal aid directory): lsc.gov

- LawHelp.org: free and low-cost legal assistance by state

- Your local courthouse self-help center: most courthouses maintain offices to assist self-represented litigants with forms, procedures, and filing requirements

Financial Planning and Tax Resources

- Institute for Divorce Financial Analysts (CDFA directory): institutedfa.com

- American Institute of Certified Public Accountants: aicpa.org

- Association of Certified Fraud Examiners: acfe.com

- IRS Publication 504: Divorced or Separated Individuals (free download from irs.gov)

- National Association of Personal Financial Advisors: napfa.org

Communication and Co-Parenting Platforms

- OurFamilyWizard: ourfamilywizard.com — court-admissible co-parenting communication platform

- TalkingParents: talkingparents.com — timestamped, unalterable messaging for co-parents

- AppClose: appclose.com — co-parenting app with scheduling and expense tracking

- Cozi Family Organizer: cozi.com — shared calendar and scheduling for families

Mental Health and Therapeutic Support

- Psychology Today Therapist Directory: psychologytoday.com/us/therapists (searchable by specialization including divorce and family issues)

- National Alliance on Mental Illness (NAMI): nami.org — support groups, education, and advocacy

- SAMHSA National Helpline: 1-800-662-4357 (substance abuse and mental health referrals, free, confidential, 24/7)

- BetterHelp / Talkspace: online therapy platforms offering flexible access to licensed therapists
- National Alliance for Eating Disorders Helpline: 1-866-662-1235

Domestic Violence Resources

- National Domestic Violence Hotline: 1-800-799-7233 (SAFE) — 24/7, confidential, multilingual
- National Domestic Violence Hotline website: thehotline.org
- National Coalition Against Domestic Violence: ncadv.org
- WomensLaw.org: legal information and resources for survivors of domestic violence
- Love Is Respect (ages 13–26): loveisrespect.org or text LOVEIS to 22522

Substance Abuse Treatment and Recovery

- SAMHSA Treatment Locator: findtreatment.gov
- Alcoholics Anonymous: aa.org
- Narcotics Anonymous: na.org
- Al-Anon Family Groups (for family members): al-anon.org
- Soberlink (remote alcohol monitoring): soberlink.com

Parenting and Child-Focused Resources

- American Academy of Child and Adolescent Psychiatry: aacap.org — resources on children and divorce

- Children in Between: online co-parenting education course accepted by many courts
- Sesame Street in Communities (divorce resources for young children): sesamestreetincommunities.org
- The Center for Divorce Education: divorce-education.com
- KidsInTheHouse.com: video-based expert parenting advice including divorce-specific content

Military-Specific Resources

- Military OneSource: militaryonesource.mil — free legal, financial, and counseling support for servicemembers and families
- Armed Forces Legal Assistance: legal aid offices on every military installation
- Defense Finance and Accounting Service (DFAS): dfas.mil — military pension division and pay information
- National Military Family Association: militaryfamily.org

Recommended Reading

- Splitting: Protecting Yourself While Divorcing Someone with Borderline or Narcissistic Personality Disorder — Bill Eddy and Randi Kreger
- BIFF: Quick Responses to High-Conflict People — Bill Eddy
- Co-Parenting with a Toxic Ex — Amy J.L. Baker and Paul R. Fine
- The Custody Evaluation Handbook — Barry Bricklin

- Divorce Poison: How to Protect Your Family from Bad-Mouthing and Brainwashing — Dr. Richard A. Warshak

- Between Two Homes: A Coparenting Handbook — Dr. Edward Teyber

ABOUT THE AUTHOR

STEPHEN RUE, ESQ.

Stephen Rue has spent nearly four decades in family law courtrooms. Over the course of his career, his law firm has handled approximately 5,000 family law cases—from uncontested dissolutions resolved in a single conference to multi-year, high-conflict custody and property battles tried before judges across multiple jurisdictions.

Licensed in Louisiana, Stephen has practiced in courtrooms where the stakes range from modest households dividing their first home to complex estates involving business valuations, forensic accounting investigations, and custody disputes spanning state and international borders.

His practice has produced a particular insight: the clients who fare best in divorce are not the ones with the strongest legal positions. They are the ones who understand the system, prepare thoroughly, control their emotions, and present their cases with the specificity and composure that judges trust. The clients who fare worst are the ones who enter the process uninformed, emotionally reactive, and dependent on assumptions that the legal system does not share.

The Winning Divorce and Custody Series was born from that insight. These books are the preparation that every client deserves— the knowledge that experienced family lawyers carry but rarely have the time to teach in full during the compressed, expensive hours of legal representation.

For more information, visit stephenrue.live

ABOUT THE COMPANION VOLUME

WINNING HIGH-CONFLICT CUSTODY BATTLES

*A Trial Lawyer's Proven Front-Line Strategies
to Protect Your Children and Your Case*

By Stephen Rue, Esq.

If your divorce involves a contested custody dispute—particularly one involving a high-conflict personality, alienation, substance abuse, domestic violence, or a complex parenting arrangement—the companion volume provides the comprehensive, deep-dive guidance that this book's custody chapters introduce.

What the Companion Volume Covers in Full Depth:

- Custody evaluations: preparation strategies, evaluator psychology, and how to present yourself authentically

- Parenting plans: advanced drafting techniques for high-conflict situations, including impasse-breaking mechanisms

- Parallel parenting: the complete operational framework for co-parenting when communication is toxic

- Parental alienation: identification, documentation, forensic evaluation, and courtroom presentation strategies

- Custody-specific courtroom testimony: extensive Q&A models for every custody issue
- Custody scripts and templates: communication scripts, documentation templates, and co-parenting protocols
- GALs, parenting coordinators, and reunification therapy: working with every court-appointed professional

Available in hardback, paperback, and e-book wherever books are sold.

THE MUST BOOK PRESS
Personal Development Series

Winning Divorce is part of the Must Book Press catalog—a publishing initiative dedicated to equipping individuals with expert knowledge in the areas where preparation matters most. Our titles deliver the practical, field-tested guidance that professionals spend careers accumulating, translated into language that real people can apply under real-world pressure.

The Winning Divorce and Custody Series by Stephen Rue, Esq.

- ***Winning Divorce****: Your Strategy for Protecting Your Children, Your Money, and Your Property in Court*
- ***Winning High-Conflict Custody Battles:*** *A Trial Lawyer's Proven Front-Line Strategies to Protect Your Children and Your Case*

stephenrue.live

THANK YOU, AND NEXT STEPS

If this book has encouraged or helped you, **would you take a moment to leave a review**? Your feedback makes a real difference and helps other readers discover this work. You can share your thoughts on Amazon.com, Goodreads.com, Barnes & Noble, or your preferred bookseller, and consider sharing or gifting this book to someone who might benefit from it.

Thank you
Stephen Rue, Esq.